How To Publicize High Tech Products & Services
By Daniel S. Janal

Meet the Author

Daniel Janal is a nationally known speaker, trainer, consultant and author. He has spoken at many conventions, including those sponsored by the Software Publishers Association, Apple Computer and Commodore International. He also has presented marketing workshops for the Public Relations Society of America, Speakers USA and the Learning Annex.

As founder of Janal Communications, a public relations agency, he has consulted with more than 50 hardware and software companies since 1982, including Grolier Electronic Publishing, Prentice Hall Home Software and QuantumLink (now America Online!).

An award winning newspaper reporter and editor, Mr. Janal received his bachelor's and master's degrees in Journalism from the famed Medill School of Journalism at Northwestern University. He also served as news editor and business editor for Gannett Newspapers in upstate New York. He received awards from the Hearst Foundation, National Education Association-Florida Teaching Profession and the Greater Orlando Press Club.

Mr. Janal is available to conduct his results-oriented marketing and management seminars for companies. He also continues to consult with companies that need to raise their visibility. For a free initial consultation, please call 408-734-2092.

How to Publicize High Tech Products and Services: A Hands-on Guide
Copyright (c) 1991-92 by Daniel S. Janal
All rights reserved
First edition, second printing

Library of Congress Cataloging in Publication Data
Janal, Daniel S.
      How to Publicize High Tech Products and Services: A Hands-on Guide
      First edition, second printing
1. Marketing. 2. Public Relations 3. Computers
CIP90-092252
      CIP
ISBN: 1-879572-00-1

Printed in the United States of America

Learn Publicity
Guaranteed

"How to Publicize High Tech Products and Services" is a 180-page workbook filled with successful strategies, worksheets and samples from leading industry companies. You'll learn all the elements to create a productive publicity campaign that can generate sales and leads.

PR pro Dan Janal teaches you to:

- Write effective press releases
- Talk to reporters
- Position products for editors
- Publicize products at trade shows
- and much, much more.

Perfect for:
- Novice PR agents
- Managers dealing with publicity
- Getting more from your agency
- Seeing what works for other companies

"Even sophisticated publicists are likely to find a good many fresh ideas here."

Jeff Tarter
Soft-letter

Table of Contents

Section 1

A Hands-On Approach to Public Relations

Chapter 1 - Build a Strong PR Plan

Chapter 2 - Tools of the Trade

Chapter 3 - Targeting the Media

Chapter 4 - Getting the Word Out

Section 2

Conventional Wisdom:
How to Publicize Products and Services at Conventions

Chapter 1 - What to Do Before the Show

Chapter 2 - What to Do at the Show

Chapter 3 - Maximize Your Exposure

Chapter 4 - How to Follow up

Section 3

How to Hire, Fire and Inspire an Agency

Chapter 1 - Client/Agency Relations

Dedication

To my clients, the best people on the face of the earth.

To the reporters, for all they do.

Acknowledgements

Lynne Marcus and Leslie Nassau - eagle-eyed copy editors with a command of the King's English and boundless enthusiasm.

Kevin Wells for an excellent design job.

Peggy Watt, Scott Mace, Mark Brownstein and Michael Miller of InfoWorld, Bill Howard, Robin Raskin and Matt Ross of PC Magazine, Chris Shipley, David DeJean and Greg Jarboe of PC Computing, Jeff Tarter of Soft*Letter, Larry Shannon and Peter Lewis of the New York Times, Stephen Banker of PCTV, Selby Bateman and Lance Elko of Signal Research, Bernie Theobald, Cliff Karnes and Pete Scisco of Compute, Keith Ferrell of Omni, Ted Needleman of Computers in Accounting, "Dr." John Heilborn, Mike Himowitz of the Baltimore Sun, Charlie Cooper and Michael Banks of Computer Shopper, Jeff Silverstein and Maureen Fleming of Digital Information Group, Mike Comeduhl of PC Resource, Dennis Allen and Rich Malloy of Byte, Dave Needle of Computer Currents, Dana Blankenhorn of Teleputing Hotline, Walter Salm of Atlantic Tech, Stewart Alsop of PC Letter, Charlie Bowen of CompuServe and Esther Dyson of RElease 1.0.

Betty Skov of Logitech, Beverly McDonald, Peter Baron, Robert Snowden Jones and Pam Alexander of Alexander Communications, Pat Meier of Pat Meier and Associates, Shel Israel of Shel Israel Public Relations, Jodi Pollock of the Software Publishers Association, Steve Leon of Technopolis Communications and Michael Cahlin of Cahlin/Williams Communications, Susan Morrow of DACeasy. Lee Levitt of PRSA, Joel Strasser of Dorf and Stanton, Dan Sussman of Burson Marstellar and Alan Penchansky. Jodi Pollock, Katherine Borsecnick, Peter Beruk and Ken Wasch of the Software Publishers Association. Rachael Paddock of the Association of Desk-Top Publishers.

Greg Doench of Prentice-Hall, John Cole of Datapro, Marylyn Rosenblum and Dave Arganbright of Grolier Electronic Publishing, Howard Zack and Betty Chancellor of Clark Boardman, Thom Henderson, Irene Henderson, Andy Foray, CJ Wang and Ed Kang of System Enhancement Associates, Frank Tzeng of ECA Computer and Communications Products, Bob Kenney and Tom McNamara of MBS+K, Michel Prompt of Metasys, Steve Case of Quantum Computer Services, Jonathan Wallace of Pencom, Ken Skier of SkiSoft Publishing Corporation, and Larry Parks of Productivity Software International. George Thibault of Revolution Software.

Stuart Gruber, Len and Susan Zandrow, Steve Kessler, Chet Greenspan. Sharyn Fitzpatrick for all that jazz. Dan Gutman, Tom Stitt, and Mark McDonough, true friends.

Foreword

It's a legitimate debate topic these days, from the watering holes of Palo Alto to the glass offices of Wall Street: Is the personal computer industry losing its ability to innovate?

Take up this discussion with anybody in the business and you'll quickly be swept into talk of management theory, trade and antitrust policy, and our educational system. You'll hear tirades about patent and copyright laws. You'll find ambivalence about the impact of venture capital and the public equity markets. You'll encounter all the extremes of optimism and pessimism about our economic system and our national culture. In short, you'll discover a personal computer business that has finally encountered the real world.

But an even more vexing problem faces most PC product marketers. And it's convincing many in the industry that we have a demand-side problem that eclipses any supply-side problem the industry may have.

For ten years, new innovations and new products have been thrust at the PC marketplace at a rate that far exceeds the user community's ability to absorb them. The product flow continues unabated: a recent issue of PC Week for example, contained 56 new product announcements and advance word of 15 others-all in a single summer week.

The result is a battle far more challenging than the fight for shelf space at the Egghead store. It's a struggle for space in the user's mind. And it is a struggle which leaves many outstanding new products unable to stand up and make the kind of impression necessary to achieve high-volume sales. Successful products have several things in common:

First, successful products are good products. (You can't teach a pig to fly.)

Second, these products deliver a clear and obvious benefit to the user which is easy to articulate and recognize.

Third, successful products are easy to learn and adopt.

All of these are necessary but not sufficient conditions for success. The most successful products are able to cultivate a climate of favorable opinion about them. Word of their merit spreads like a wildfire among the user community, and they quickly gain champions who promote the product to others in ways that are more powerful and effective than any member of a vendor's salesforce could possibly be. Strong word-of-mouth endorsement by opinion-leading users is, quite simply, the single most powerful determinant of product success.

Research has shown that in addition to word of mouth endorsement, significant contributors in creating a climate of favorable opinion are computer publications.

Computer publications reach an average of well over 2 million primary subscribers each month. On average, these subscribers receive more than two publications each. They each spend as much as three hours per month devouring the editorial and advertising material. In many cases, they pass these publications along to two or more people in their organization. Better than a half-million computer magazines are bought on the newsstand each month. Computer publications are the principal source of information about products in the marketplace today and a battleground for first impressions.

One of the biggest mistakes companies make, though, is stopping with the first impressions. With months of preparation going into an elaborate product launch, it's all too easy to treat the debut as the end of a process, rather than as a beginning. But the key to successfully managing the climate of opinion around a product is to constantly and consistently reinforce the impressions of a product made at launch. Without that constant reinforcement in a product's first year — and even beyond — it can easily be forgotten and lost in the noise of the next big product launch.

"How To Publicize High Tech Products and Services" draws on a wealth of experiences in the incredibly challenging personal computer business to create a highly practical guide to breaking through and reinforcing product messages. These are the foundations for any good product marketing program — prerequisites for any advertising program, retail promotion, direct-mail effort, or sales force initiative. It is a book about making the benefits of a product clear and obvious to prospective customers, through those who will write about those benefits. It is a book about fighting for attention, and about keeping people's attention once you've gotten it in the first place. Ultimately, it is a roadmap through a process that will give the best of our industry's innovative efforts a fighting chance.

Michael E. Kolowich Publisher, PC/Computing

Michael E. Kolowich is the founding publisher of PC/Computing, the largest-circulation monthly computer publication in the market today. He was corporate vice-president of marketing at Lotus Development Corporation during that company's major growth period, and was vice-president and partner at Bain and Company, a strategy consulting firm.

Preface: The Value of Publicity

Publicity is the most cost-effective marketing tool in the technology marketplace. Public relations produced a hefty 235 percent return on investment according to chief economic officers across the country who were polled by the International Association of Business Communicators Research Foundation.

Results of a survey conducted by *Soft•Letter,* a newsletter covering trends in the computer software industry, show "the software industry as a whole has come to rely heavily on public relations as a marketing tool. Especially in smaller companies, PR is likely to be a major investment area and is often viewed as a low-cost alternative to magazine advertising."

Publicity is important because it is the only part of the marketing program that builds credibility, which companies need to rise above their competitors in the technology industries which are blessed with innovative, yet unknown, start-up companies. Credibility is the key to winning the consumers' minds, hearts and pocketbooks.

When *PC Magazine* columnist John Dvorak wrote about a software utility, AXE from System Enhancement Associates, hundreds of people ordered the product. A mail order company offered to sell the product for the small publisher.

When *PC Week* columnist Jim Seymour praised Revolution Software's VGA Dimmer, a software program that saves the screen from burning out, readers jammed the phone lines with orders for several weeks.

When *New York Times* writer Peter Lewis wrote about Eye Relief, a large type word processor from SkiSoft Publishing Corporation, the article was syndicated to 12 newspapers in large cities, leading to orders from around the country.

When *InfoWorld* wrote about Nanometrics, the value of the company increased by approximately $1 million.

Commodore International introduced the Amiga Computer in 1985, the registration cards showed that 87 percent of the early buyers said they bought the computer based on public relations in the form of reviews and news articles they had read. PR was far more effective than the other choices: advertising and salespersons' suggestions. Although we can debate that product's success, it is clear that publicity drove early sales.

Advertising, direct mail and the advice of salespersons have long been viewed as the most effective ways to sell high tech products. However, in the high tech marketplace, public relations commands respect because it can increase sales and support advertising, direct mail and sales. Public relations differs from advertising in that advertising controls the message, while PR does not. Because of this distinction, PR creates credibility. Advertising can't create credibility. When readers see the ad, they sometimes think "Big deal, that's what THEY say." Skeptical readers are more apt to believe independent authorities such as reporters, columnists, reviewers or broadcasters who lend credibility to products and services in their newspaper columns, magazine reviews and television shows. These writers were influenced by public relations methods.

Public relations helps advertising by creating credibility for the product. For example, credibility is built when an ad quotes reviewers extolling the product's virtues or includes an emblem proclaiming the product as the "Product of the Year" according to a leading publication. Public relations helps a company win awards by creating awareness.

PR also helps direct mail sales and in-person sales by providing credible sales collateral material such as brochures, advertisements, flyers and point of purchase displays. These collateral pieces can take the form of reprints of positive reviews, excerpts from those reviews and testimonials from users. These exhibits go a long way to building credibility for your company and its products.

Publicity does not exist in a corporate vacuum. The publicity department should coordinate activities with the marketing, advertising, direct mail and sales departments to ensure that one consistent message is delivered to the customer.

This book will show you how to create a positive impression with reporters on the phone, in person, through the mail and at trade shows. You will learn how to position your company, products and services so that reporters will want to write about them.

This is a great challenge. The number of companies seeking publicity is great, while the number of editorial pages in magazines is small. Many products – even the most deserving – do not get reviewed in the leading publications. After reading this book and completing the exercises, you will have a better idea of how to rise above the noise level to ensure that your products or services have the best chances of getting reviewed. Unlike other books about publicity, this book strives to present an innovative publicity program that you can implement immediately.

Section 1 presents a complete workshop to help you think like a public relations professional. By following the exercises, you will learn how to position your company, products or services, write a authoritative press release and deliver a professional phone pitch — the essential tools of high tech public relations.

Section 2 focuses on how to attract publicity at trade shows, which we believe are the single best opportunity for young, growing companies with tight budgets to get attention. You can implement many strategies discussed in this book without renting expensive booth space at national shows. Reporters will write about products from the smallest companies if those products are innovative and presented to the press properly.

Section 3 helps you hire, fire and inspire a public relations agency.

After you read this book, you should understand how to develop a public relations program that can effectively promote your products and services. Good luck.

Who Should Read This Book

This book can help make money and save time for:

- Publicity professionals seeking new tactics and strategies.
- Entrepreneurs needing to publicize products and services.
- Beginning publicity professionals who wants to improve skills.
- International marketers unfamiliar with the United States press and its practices.
- Public relations students.
- Marketing managers who must understand the publicist's role.
- Senior public relations executives who need a training manual for new hires.
- High tech service providers who must improve marketing.

The book provides a variety of answers to your needs. It presents:

- Strategies and rationales for programs and step-by-step recipes for executing those plans
- Workshop techniques - fill in the blank questions - to help you improve your skills and refine your thinking
- Checklists, sample press releases, backgrounders, profiles, case histories, letters, forms and flyers to use as a starting point .

Whenever possible, we have quoted experts, publicity professionals, technology reporters and analysts in actual situations. A case history approach lets you learn from the triumphs and tragedies of the best minds in the business.

Publicity is a problem – solving vehicle. Because situations continually change, so will this book, which we will update regularly. We welcome your suggestions on topics that should be included. We also welcome your strategies and tactics. Please call or write me with your comments.

Dan Janal
Janal Communications

SECTION 1

A Hands-on Approach To Public Relations

Many tools exist to help you

publicize products. This

section and its worksheets will

help you decide which ones

are right for you so you can

create the unique messages

that meet your needs.

How to Gain Credibility: Tell the Truth

When reporters discover bad news, what should you tell them?

The truth.

The press is bound to find out about a major problem. If you lie or try to hide it, you will kill your number– one asset – your credibility. You might even gain credibility if you bring the problem to their attention.

Here's how to make the best of a bad situation. When a reporter calls with bad news, follow these steps:

- Acknowledge the problem.
- Explain how the problem is being corrected.
- Tell reporters you will keep them updated.
- Ask if they have any other questions.
- Offer to let them speak to company executives.
- Don't lie, hide the truth, or obscure the facts.

If you follow these steps, reporters will cooperate with you. If you don't, they'll treat you like a leper. Telling the truth is a cardinal rule in life and it should be one in PR. Good PR people don't tell lies because they know lies will come back to haunt them. Similarly, good bosses and clients don't ask PR people to lie for them.

Get Your Message Across ■

In the battle to get high tech PR, you don't have the luxury of rambling. Too many competing products are fighting for too little editorial space. You need a road map to help you reach your destination — getting the favorable attention of the reporter.

Let's do a few exercises to help clarify your thinking and put it into a framework the reporter will expect.

These exercises will help you:

- Determine your message.
- Understand what information the press wants.
- Create press kits to deliver your message.
- Create cover letters and phone pitches to deliver your message.
- Help you understand the variety of editorial opportunities and how best to take advantage of them.
- Select the media to whom you should tell your message.
- Decide which vehicle you should use to disseminate the message (press conference, interviews, hospitality suites, etc.).
- Determine the action you want reporters to take (write news articles, product reviews, industry analysis articles).
- Get psyched to call reporters and meet new people.

If you complete these exercises, you will begin reaching your goal of presenting a professional image to the press.

Set Clear Objectives ■

When Greg Jarboe was the publicity director at Lotus, he had an idea that would enable the company to create excitement. The concept was a trade fair called Lotus Week that would feature product announcements, demonstrations and meetings among company leaders and leading customers.

But first he had to justify the program. "If I wanted to spend millions of dollars, I had to show what those dollars would buy," Jarboe said. To do this, he wrote a plan that projected sales and news stories that would be written to help marketing.

The point is that he set goals. When Lotus Week was over, he could compare the results to the goals and see if the program was a success. Based on his plan and budget, the idea was approved. Lotus Week was such a success that the company has held the fair every year, even though Jarboe has left Lotus to become marketing director for PC Computing Magazine.

By setting goals, you will be able to measure your publicity plan's success. Let's set a goal right now.

You can measure publicity goals several ways. Publicity can:

- Increase sales.
- Make you famous.
- Provide sales collateral material in the form of reviews and news.
- Publicize your products.
- Increase the price of company stock.
- Lead to co-marketing and distribution arrangements.
- Create opportunities for strategic alliances.
- Get your company sold to the highest bidder.
- Create visibility overseas.
- Make your product an overnight sensation.
- Make an old product look new.
- Make a new product look established (not old!).
- Create a new product category.
- Make you look so good, the boss promotes you.
- Make an executive look so good, he or she is hired by another company.

Publicity can help you reach ego goals, financial goals and sales goals. Which goals do you want to reach? Write the goal you want to achieve on the Goal Setting Worksheet on the next page. You might want to copy the page before writing on it, so you can have clean pages for future projects.

My primary goal for publicity is:

_____

_____

_____

Let's see if that goal is realistic. To determine that, you'll need to determine:

- The time you think is necessary to reach that goal.
- The amount of money needed to reach that goal.
- Some numbers associated with that goal, so you'll know you have achieved it. For instance, you might want 10 reviews in computer magazines in six months and you have a $10,000 budget. Or you might want to increase executives' exposure by placing them on five panels at computer shows and you have a $1,000 budget and a six-month time frame.
- Specific numbers. If you say "some reviews" in "any magazine" you are setting imprecise standards. Do you want to get 10 reviews or 50? Do you want to increase sales by 10 percent or 20 percent?

If any elements are missing from your goal statement, you won't know if you have met your goals. If you have definite, realistic goals, then you have created accountability that can determine the program's success and justify approval from top management.

Before committing to your goal, be realistic. Remember, you will be held accountable if you don't achieve the targets. If you haven't budgeted enough time or money, you might miss the mark and feel crushed. You need to set goals that you can reach. When you reach these goals, you'll feel good. Then you can set new, higher goals. Let's continue this exercise.

By using this goal worksheet, you'll be able to judge whether your program is a success. If you hire a public relations agency, you can use this goal worksheet to set targets for the agency. The PR agency should welcome this, as they will then know how they will be judged. If they meet the goal, they can assume you are happy. If they don't reach the goal, they won't complain when you fire them.

Goal Setting Worksheet

1. My primary goal is:

   _____

   _____

   _____

   _____

2. How much time will I need to reach that goal?

   _____

   _____

   _____

3. How much money will I need to reach that goal?

   _____

   _____

   _____

4. How can I quantify results so I know I've reached that goal?

   _____

   _____

   _____

Determine Your Message

Bill Howard, PC Magazine's executive editor, stood at the podium of a panel at the Software Publishers Association and held a dollar bill in front of his face. He let it slip from his fingers. It floated gracefully to the floor in about 10 seconds.

"That is how much time you have to catch an editor's attention," he said.

Although 10 seconds is not a lot of time, it is enough time to catch the favorable attention of an editor. For instance, the following statement might describe your product:

- The X-25 board makes any Macintosh computer run faster.

A reporter can relate to that and will talk to you about it. And it took only nine words.

Helping you condense your message so you can say it in 10 seconds is the focus of this exercise. This message is called a positioning statement. Developing a positioning statement is a key element to any successful PR program because the statement tells the world how your products differ from competitors. To develop your positioning statement, you will participate in a series of exercises that will help determine the unique characteristics of your product. Marketing gurus call this statement the Unique Selling Proposition.

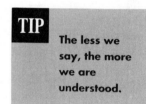

TIP

The less we say, the more we are understood.

If you have a background in management, you can compare the positioning statement to an executive summary. It describes the product in the shortest amount of time and words so even the busiest editors will listen and be able to determine if they need or want more information. For instance:

- XYZ Corporation is the leading publisher of CAD-CAM software.
- ABC Group is the largest desktop publishing service bureau in New York.

These are good statements because they tell what the companies do and what positions they hold in their marketplaces.

The positioning statement is the basis for your verbal and print contact with the press. You will use this statement when you talk to the press on the phone and in person. You will use it when you write and print press releases. Therefore, it is important to refine the message so it reflects your product's philosophy. It might be your only shot to attract a reporter's attention.

Because this positioning statement is so important to the company, you should give serious consideration to involving the marketing, sales and promotional departments in creating this message. By creating a team atmosphere, you will create a unified message that will reflect the needs of each major department.

Brevity is the key.

The great Broadway showman Flo Ziegfeld told an aspiring writer that if his idea couldn't fit onto a business card, then he hadn't fully developed the idea. Speech writers have long heard the anecdote that it takes two hours to write a half-hour speech, four hours to write a 15-minute speech and a day to write a five-minute speech.

Most readers have heard the earthier message "KISS" (Keep it simple, stupid.) The less we say, the more we are understood. That's because people can't comprehend long strings of information. This next exercise will help you create a message that tells the audience why they should buy your product or retain your services.

For instance, when ECA Computer & Communications Products introduced a hand-held color scanner. The writer asked three questions that helped create the positioning statement. The questions and answers are listed here:

Question: Customers will know my product is truly unique because:

Answer: It is the only one that will read 256 colors in one pass.

Question: Customers will benefit from my product because:

Answer: 1. It won't strain their budget. It costs only $699.
2. It can read and write to TIF and PCX industry standard file formats so people can use my product with the programs they use now.
3. It comes with a slide show animator program so users can take their drawings and turn them into viable presentations.

Question: My product meets the needs of these three types of users:

Answer: 1. Desktop publishers.
2. Graphic artists.
3. Home office users on a budget.

Now it is your turn. Fill in the blanks on the worksheet on the following page.

Positioning Worksheet

Users know the product is unique because it is the only one that:

A _____

2. Customers will benefit from my product because:

A _____

B _____

C _____

3. My product meets the needs of these three types of users:

A _____

B _____

C _____

You now need to test tnese samples. Read them out loud. Do the words roll off your tongue? Good. Are they tongue twisters? Try again. If you develop a strong, positive pitch now, you'll sound like an expert when you talk to reporters.

Now read these questions and answers to two people in your office, preferably people who are not familiar with the product. Then ask if they can explain, in their own words, what the product does and who should use it. If they can, you have a hit. If not, try again. Don't ask a question that can be answered "yes" or "no." People will always say "yes" to avoid embarrassment.

TIP Test your positioning statement.

You have just completed the first exercise in creating a positioning statement. You'll take this material and mold other message in the next chapters.

Produce Sound Bites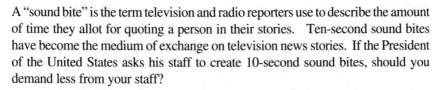

A "sound bite" is the term television and radio reporters use to describe the amount of time they allot for quoting a person in their stories. Ten-second sound bites have become the medium of exchange on television news stories. If the President of the United States asks his staff to create 10-second sound bites, should you demand less from your staff?

Let's take the information you created in the last chapter and whittle it down to a 10-second sound bite. (Don't toss out the rest of the material, we'll use it later in the press release.) Your sound bite will be the foundation for your phone pitch, press release and in-person demo. Yet it will occupy the back space of a business card.

First, think like a reporter. Reporters want to grab a reader's attention. Therefore, think in terms of readers. What will benefit them?

Take the most important point — as it relates to the reader — and use conventional journalistic style. Answer the basic journalistic questions of: who, what, when, why, where and how. Here are some examples:

> ECA C&C Products today introduced the first hand-held scanner capable of reading 256 colors in one pass. (18 words)

> Designers and desktop publishers can now scan 256 colors with one pass by using a new scanner introduced today by ECA C&C Products. (23 words)

These examples tell reporters and readers what is new about the product and who can use it. It is useful to create this summary because:

- It might be the only thing reporters read.
- It might be the only thing they write in a news brief digest.

Here is an example of what NOT to do:

> The most revolutionary, state-of-the-art product that will change the way people work is being developed by Camouflage Technologies.

This example uses cliches that will raise red flags for editors who get so many press releases claiming their products are the biggest and best, fastest and easiest to use, next generation and truly revolutionary, that the words become meaningless. Instead of using cliches, tell what makes your product unique. If it is unique, reporters will know.

As Stephen Banker, a television technology journalist says, "Don't tell me what's news. It is up to me to do my job and find out if it is news."

Sound Bite Worksheet

Following the examples on the previous page, write two samples for your product.

1 _____

_____

_____

_____

_____

_____

_____

2 _____

_____

_____

_____

_____

_____

_____

Submit these samples to the "read aloud" test and the "peer listening" test. Upgrade your paragraphs and test again.

Create Your Company Position

You've described the unique aspect of your product in the previous exercise. Now let's work on a positioning statement for your company. A company positioning statement describes the company's main mission in a very few words.

For example, say Widget World is the leading manufacturer of widgets for the government marketplace. Little-known companies want to create a positioning statement so editors and readers will get to know them better. Editors might not be familiar with Widget World. But they will become familiar with the company if they read that Widget World is the major producer of widgets.

Fill out the worksheet on the following page. Then practice reading the statement aloud until it sounds right. Then get feedback from people in your office.

This statement is the basis for your verbal and print contact with reporters. You will use this statement when you talk to the press on the phone and in person. and when you write press releases. Your advertising department will also tie this theme to its work. The more you use this statement, the more it will become ingrained in people's minds. When people see Widget World, they will immediately think of the major producer of widgets.

Company Positioning Worksheet

These exercises will help you create a positioning statement for your company.

Think for a minute. What image do you want to pop into people's minds when they hear your company's name? Write three things that come to mind.

1 _____

_____

_____

_____

2 _____

_____

_____

_____

3 _____

_____

_____

_____

Which of those three statements is the one that clearly identifies your company?

_____

_____

_____

Cut a few words and make it even shorter.

_____

Press Kits Tell Your Story

Let's look at the tools of trade: the press kit and its components. Once you understand what reporters look for and how they communicate, you will have the opportunity to take the message you created and weave it into a press release. Please note that your company might not use all these materials. Choose the ones you feel are necessary.

Press Kits

A press kit communicates your message in detail to reporters. It can contain these elements:

- Press release - a two or three page announcement stating the benefits, features, marketing and system requirements of the new product.

- Case histories - testimonials from satisfied users told in the "how to" form, describing how a company or person overcame a problem by using your product orservice.

- Backgrounder – the company's history, a description of its products and profiles of founders and managers.

- Fact sheets – encapsulated company highlights.

- Reviewers guidelines – highlights of features that reviewers should look for.

- Response card – postage-paid response card for reporters to send to you asking for product, photos or more information.

- Photographs – color and black-and-white shots of the product or person. Software companies should include pictures of several screens.

This section will explore each of these materials, provide samples and let you write your own.

Write Effective Press Releases

A press release is a descriptive marketing tool that tells the press what is new, interesting and exciting about your product or service. It also tells how your product compares with others and includes marketing information. You'll have a chance to explore these topics in the workshop section and write your own press release.

Reporters get hundreds of press releases a day so they don't have time to read them all from beginning to end. Therefore, a press release should rarely be longer than two pages. Unless you work for a top-tier company in your market, reporters rarely will read longer press releases. Use 8 1/2 by 11 inch paper. To increase legibility, use 1 1/2 or double spacing.

Let's examine a press release's elements. Then you'll have a chance to write one.

To catch the reporter's interest, you must follow a distinct format. Print your press release on company letterhead. Some press releases say "news release" or "press release." These words are not necessary because a press release has a distinct format, just as poems or screenplays have distinct layouts and designs.

Every press release should contain the release date and contact person's names, titles and phone numbers just below the letterhead on the left margin. The name of the public relations agency, if there is one, can go alongside or underneath. Include the executive's desk phone (this will speed calls past the switchboard), home phone (because the press works under tight deadlines and might need to contact the executive after normal business hours) and MCI Mail account.

TIP

You can save time by creating a file for this heading. When you write a new press release, you can recall it into your new text instantly.

You can save time by creating a file for this heading. When you write a new press release, you can recall it into your new text instantly.

Every press release must have a headline that defines the press release's main point. It may be followed by sub-heads, which illustrate secondary points.

Press Contacts:

Frank Tzeng
Associate President
ECA C&C Products
(office) 201-555-1213
(home) 201-555-1214
MCI Mail: 123-457

Daniel Janal
President
Janal Communications
(office) 201-555-2345
(home) 201-555-3456
MCI Mail: 123-456

ECA Ships First Hand-held Scanner to Read 256 Colors
Targeted for Desktop Publishers, Home Office Users
Compatible with All Standard File Formats

LODI, NJ — April 16, 1990 — The first hand-held scanner to read 256 colors
in one pass and write those files to industry standard TIF and PCX formats
is being shipped today by ECA Computer and Communications Products.
Designed for home-office and desktop publishers, the IBM PC compatible
product sells for $350 and is compatible with all industry file formats.

For legibility, center headlines. A blank line should separate each line for easy
readability. The first letter of each word could be capitalized to make the headline
even more distinctive. DO NOT print the entire headline in hard-to-read capital
letters. **IMAGINE READING A HEADLINE THAT LOOKED LIKE THIS.
DIFFICULT, ISN'T IT?**

The first paragraph begins with a dateline, which consists of the city and state where
the company is located and the date of the release. The body copy follows
immediately.

LODI, NJ, — April 16, 1990 — The first hand-held...

TIP

Use upper and lower case letters in a headline to increase legibility.

If you are distributing the press release at a convention, you
should use the name of that city in the dateline. Follow it with
the date and the first paragraph. The lead paragraph is a quick
encapsulation of the main message of the release. It should
answer the questions: who, what, when, where, why and how.

If this press release is timed for a trade show, include the name of the show and the company's booth number.   That lead would now read:

> ATLANTA — April 16, 1990 — The first hand-held scanner to read 256 colors in one pass and write those files to industry standard TIF and PCX formats is now being shipped by ECA Computer and Communications Products.   Designed for home-office and desktop publishers, the IBM PC compatible product sells for $350 and is compatible with all industry file formats.   It is being demonstrated at Comdex/Spring in Booth 2211.

One of the newest techniques to grab the editor's attention is to begin the press release with an executive summary.   Notice how the press release for DeScribe contains a headline as in a traditional release.   The executive summary follows in bold type with both margins indented.   Information about the new features, benefits, prices and positioning.   The press release then continues with background information on the product and the technology.   Whenever you write a press release about a new technology, describe the information in non-technical terms. Use analogies, examples and definitions to make yourself understood.

The press release announcing this book uses the scholar's outline, that is, two uneven columns.   This format allows editors to scan the page easily.

Another innovative design is the "routing slip" printed onto the PSI press release. This format effectively suggests that editors send the release to the appropriate person.   You would send the release to the beat reporter.   If he or she knows of another editor working on a story who could use the information, you might get another mention of your product or service.

Traditional press releases, showing good form and function are presented by The Cobb Group and General Information.

Press releases use two style markers to signify the end of each page and the end of the final page.   To alert reporters that another page follows, the center bottom of each page should have the word "more" printed inside a pair of dashes:

– more –

The final page should print these symbols centered after the last paragraph, which tell the reporter that the press release is ending:

###

To draw attention, hightight selected sentences with a yellow marker.

Look at these samples and then answer the questions in the worksheet to produce a professional looking and sounding press release.

494 ? North Freeway Boulevard
Sacramento, CA 95834
FAX/923 3447
916/646-1111

Agency Contact: Pat Meier
Pat Meier Associates, Inc.
123 Townsend, Suite 102
San Francisco, CA 94107
(415) 957-5999

Company Contact: Clif Whalen
(916) 646-1111

For Immediate Release

NEW RELEASE OF DESCRIBE BRINGS POWERFUL MULTI-USER WORD PUBLISHING FEATURES TO LAN USERS

Sacramento, CA - September 10, 1990 - The new DeScribe™ - Word Publisher, version 2.0, LAN software delivers all the features of DeScribe's popular single-user product to networked systems.

Enhanced DDE (Dynamic Data Exchange) allows DeScribe 2.0 to act as a DDE server. Hot Link DeScribe text from one character to entire documents to other OS/2 packages or to other DeScribe documents.

DeScribe Inc. announced today it has shipped its latest word publishing package, DeScribe™ - Word Publisher 2.0 which supports multiple users on local area networks.

Client and server packages   DeScribe™-Word Publisher (DWP) is available in server and client packages. The server package, which contains all of the word publishing and network software for DeScribe and a license for one user, can either be installed on a network server for multiple users or on a stand-alone workstation for individual use. Each client package contains a license for one additional user and one copy of the documentation.

Public Relations Pat Meier Associates, Inc., 123 Townsend Street, Suite 102 San Francisco, CA 94107, Telephone 415/957-5999; Fax 415/957-1733

KAHUNA monitors users

The DeScribe Kahuna program monitors the number of concurrent users of DeScribe for the network's system administrator. Kahuna guarantees that the number of concurrent users of DeScribe does not exceed the number of user licenses installed on that network. The system administrator can increase the program's limits as additional client licenses are purchased.

Network services

DWP 2.0 allows system administrators to define system dictionaries, layouts, and macros for shared use by all users on a network. This provides a shared environment for the work group and simplifies the task of creating a consistent image in documents produced by the group.

Dynamic Data Exchange Enhancements

DeScribe's already powerful Dynamic Data Exchange (DDE) capabilities have been augmented so that DeScribe can work as either a server or client in DDE conversations. Any amount of text or graphics can be assigned a tag name. Tagged data can be controlled directly by the user to forge DDE hot links with other applications or be totally automated using DeScribe Macro Language.

For example, numbers in DeScribe text can be DDE linked to a spreadsheet template with a predefined formula. The spreadsheet calculates a solution which DeScribe retrieves and correctly positions in text. Change one of the tagged numbers and the answer automatically updates to the correct value.

DeScribe also brings a unique tool to DDE - export. DDE links can be forged to another application (or DeScribe itself) from within DeScribe. So, data can be exported to another application, another DeScribe document, or the same DeScribe document. The

	subtle distinction means that you work in one application instead of cutting and "paste linking" between two or more applications.
Draft Printing	New print options let users quickly print a draft copy of a document. Text is printed in a default font and size with lines of text starting at the same position as WYSIWYG printouts.
Save Custom Interfaces	DeScribe 2.0 makes it simple for clients to pass dramatically modified human interfaces to other users. This feature is of special interest to large corporations and VARs who integrate DeScribe into their vertical application.
Go To Page/Line	Allows users to move quickly to a specific page or line.

"DeScribe's Network Version 2.0 steps up to the task of addressing the needs of corporate desktop computing by providing LAN based systems support and OS/2 connectivity to large servers of mainframes."

- Allan Katzen, CEO & President of DeScribe, Inc.

For further information, contact Pat Meier Associates, Inc., 123 Townsend Street, Suite 102, San Francisco, CA 94107, phone (415) 957-5999, fax (415) 957-1733, MCI Mail 374-5221

DeScribe™ Word Publisher, the first word processor for OS/2 Presentation Manager, combines advanced word processing functions with powerful desktop publishing features and extensive drawing capabilities. Server packages (which can be loaded on stand-alone workstations for individual use) list for $595.00. Client packages list for $250. Multi-packs are available for quantity purchase. (Call SALES, DeScribe, Inc. for purchasing information.) Twenty-three foreign language, legal, medical, biographical, and scientific dictionary options are available for $149.95 each.

This press release was created and produced using the DeScribe™ - Word Publisher

PSI INTRODUCES hyperSTORE-400

New line of caching disk controllers
for IBM-and-compatible microcomputers
shatters price/performance barriers

NEWS RELEASE

Comdex booth N286,
Sands Convention Center

Attention:

❏ Operating system editors
❏ Hard-disk editors
❏ Mass storage editors
❏ Controller editors
❏ Caching editors
❏ Hardware editors
❏ Peripherals editors
❏ Computer editors
❏ New product editors
❏ Product review editors

Editors contact:

Steven J. Leon
President
Technopolis® Communications
6000 Canterbury Dr. D301
Culver City, Calif. 90230
℡ 213-670-5606
(FAX) 213-670-2064

Company contacts:

Chip Hilts
Vice president,
sales & marketing
Warren Lee
Vice president,
research & development
Perceptive Solutions Inc.
2700 Flora St.
Dallas, Tex. 75201
℡ 214-954-1774
(FAX) 214-953-1774

LAS VEGAS, Nov. 12, 1990 -- Perceptive Solutions Inc. (PSI) today introduced at Comdex/Fall '90 the *hyperSTORE-400 Series*™, a pair of caching disk controllers that shatter price barriers and throttle up to warp speed the performance of IBM-and-compatible microcomputers.

The hyperSTORE-400 Series cuts to minutes disk-bound tasks that might otherwise take hours -- including accounting, database, networking, image and voice processing, desktop publishing and engineering applications, as well as programs that require memory-intensive graphical user interfaces (GUIs), such as Windows 3.0 and X Windows.

Available in models that support the IDE and SCSI interfaces, the two hyperSTORE-400 Series controllers both retail for under $750, delivering at almost half the cost the mainframe-like caching power of PSI's advanced *hyperSTORE-1600*™.

"The hyperSTORE-400 Series of controllers shatter price barriers, making high-performance hardware disk caching affordable to a new, broad market of users," said Chip Hilts, vice president of sales and marketing for Dallas-based PSI.

Like the hyperSTORE-1600, the hyperSTORE-400 Series features average access times of 0.28 milliseconds, data transfer rates of up to 4 megabytes per second, and drop-in compatibility with all standard operating systems, including MS/PC-DOS, NetWare, Xenix, UNIX, PC-MOS, VM/386, PICK and THEOS.

Similarly, the hyperSTORE-400 Series controllers are "intelligent," with a powerful 16-bit Z280 microprocessor, and serve as a self-contained computer dedicated to mass-storage management and control. This frees the central processing unit of a personal computer, file server or workstation for other tasks, eliminating the bottleneck that chokes the flow of data between the microprocessor and the hard disk or other storage device.

Spurring the price/performance breakthrough is the one-interface, one-board design of the hyperSTORE-400, which simplifies the modular, multi-board design of the hyperSTORE-1600.

(more)

Users may readily install the hyperSTORE-400 IDE and SCSI models in one standard 16-bit ISA/EISA expansion slot, replacing the conventional hard-disk/floppy-disk controller.

In contrast, the hyperSTORE-1600 comprises an array of components and options able to support multiple interfaces and 70 configurations. Unlike the hyperSTORE-400 Series, the hyperSTORE-1600 is designed for systems integrators and value-added resellers to build and install for users.

hSOS, DataShadow

The one-interface, one-slot hyperSTORE-400 controllers feature the *hyperSTORE Operating System*™ (hSOS) -- which is also used by the hyperSTORE-1600.

The hSOS transforms the controllers into intelligent, multitasking computers able to circumvent the plodding performance of mechanical drives. Transparent to MS/PC-DOS or any other standard operating system, the hSOS controls caching functions and concurrently executes such separate operations as managing cache memory and writing to and reading from hard-disk drives.

The hSOS also supports PSI's *DataShadow*™ hardware disk mirroring, an option that enables users to create a fault-tolerant, parallel storage system.

DataShadow transparently stores data to two independent drives to protect against the loss of critical data should any one drive fail. As an added benefit, DataShadow effectively doubles data throughput by cutting physical access times in half.

With DataShadow, mirroring operations are performed entirely within the controller, without the need for device drivers. This enables users to add fault tolerance to operating systems that do not provide a mirroring option, such as MS/PC-DOS or Novell NetWare ELS.

400 Series features

The new, one-interface, one-board controllers support two floppy-disk drives and two hard-disk drives.

Under MS/PC-DOS, this provides users of the IDE model hyperSTORE-400 with up to 1GB of high-performance hard-disk storage using the largest possible IDE drives of 504MB.

Users of the hyperSTORE-400 SCSI model may gain additional mass storage under certain operating systems. For example, UNIX and Xenix enable SCSI-model users to configure systems in which the second hard drive exceeds 504MB -- as long as the first drive conforms to the requirements of the WD-1003 emulation.

When drives are mirrored under DataShadow, the hyperSTORE-400I model supports two pair of mirrored drives, for a total of 2GB storage.

4MB RAM cache

Both model controllers load frequently-used data and applications into a RAM-based cache as large as 4MB. The cache uses standard 100 nanosecond 256Kb/1Mbx9 SIMMs that users may add in pairs as needed.

For instant access to cached data, the proprietary algorithms of PSI's hSOS analyze cache contents and anticipate what data may be needed, enabling users to access data at warp speeds of 0.28ms -- almost 100 times faster than a typical 28ms hard disk.

Further, the controllers transfer up to 4MB of data per second to and from the cache. In contrast, conventional controllers and even other caching controllers transfer less than 1MB of data per second.

Both hyperSTORE-400 controllers emulate a Western Digital WD-1003 controller, which ensures compatibility with all standard operating systems.

The hyperSTORE-400S SCSI model supports SCSI-1 and SCSI-2 hard-disk drives at synchronous transfer rates of up to 5MB per second. It features a standard 50-pin internal connector. An external Macintosh-type 25-pin connector is available to support external disk subsystems.

The hyperSTORE-400I supports up to two AT/IDE hard-disk drives and transfer speeds of over 4MB per second. This model features two independent 40-pin IDE connectors, which allows support of two mirrored pairs of IDE drives -- including IDE drives from different manufacturers that are sometimes incompatible.

Availability, pricing

The hyperSTORE-400 models will be available in early 1991. Each will retail for a suggested price of $745.00, with 0K RAM. The DataShadow option retails for a suggested $270.00.

Perceptive Solutions Inc., based in Dallas, was founded in 1988. The company is a pioneer developer, manufacturer and marketer of "intelligent" caching disk controllers and related products for personal computers and workstations. ■

hyperSTORE, DataShadow, hyperSTORE Operating System, hSOS and PSI are trademarks of Perceptive Solutions Inc. All other trademarks and registered trademarks are acknowledged.

JANAL COMMUNICATIONS
MARKETING COMMUNICATIONS AND PUBLIC RELATIONS
3030 EDWIN AVENUE, SUITE 2G
FORT LEE, NEW JERSEY 07024

201-947-9839

FOR IMMEDIATE RELEASE

FOR INFORMATION: Daniel Janal
Janal Communications
201-947-9839
MCI-341-8158, JANAL
CompuServe - 76004,1046

Book Teaches Tech Firms to Improve Press Relations

SPA, PRSA, Editors Laud "How to Publicize High Tech Products and Services"

Book trains PR people

Fort Lee, NJ -- January 15, 1991 -- Software publishers and hardware manufacturers can learn to promote their products effectively and efficiently with a new book, "How to Publicize High Tech Products and Services: A Hands-On Guide" (Janal Communications, January 1991, 176 pages, $49.95, 800-933-3612 or 201-947-9839).

Worksheets help focus messages

The authoritative guidebook serves as a training tool for beginning publicists, a reference source for experienced professionals and a hands-on work book for companies who assign inexperienced persons to perform publicity chores. It also serves as an explanation to upper management to justify and evaluate public relations programs. Written by PR veteran Daniel Janal, who has represented Prentice-Hall, Grolier Electronic Publishing, Commodore, QuantumLink and Datapro, the book includes insightful anecdotes, sample materials and thought-provoking worksheets which help readers create professional materials and gain favorable attention from editors.

Benefits

The book shows users how to:
* Write press releases, backgrounders, profiles, upgrade notices, reviewers guidelines, case studies, Question and Answer sheets and other tools of the trade
* Speak effectively to reporters on the phone and at conventions
* Arrange a press tour, press conference and conference panels
* Publicize products at conventions
* Position products and services

Endorsements

The Public Relations Society of America, the industry's professional society, has endorsed the book and has ordered copies for each members of its Technology Section. The Software Publishers Association also has placed a bulk order for its members.

- more -

Testimonials   "Dan's book has more than paid for itself within a few days," said Terry
                      Kalil, Public Relations Manager, Great Plains Software. "It is playing a
                      central role in our staff training program. I recently developed a public
                      relations training course for our product marketing team and this book
                      saved me hours of research and preparation time. I've worked in PR for
                      five years and am pleasantly surprised at how many terrific, fresh ideas
                      are included in the book. We would have gladly paid five times the price
                      to get my hands on this practical realistic guide."

Editors praise   "Dan Janal describes the basic techniques of PR more comprehensively
book   than anybody else I've ever seen," said Jeffrey Tarter, Publisher, Soft-
                      Letter.

                      "This book is full of energy and sound advice that will help companies
                      get an editor's ear. It will be especially valuable for people who are just
                      starting out," said Chris Shipley, Executive Editor of PC Computing
                      Magazine.

                      "Dan Janal offers a terrific PR primer. His pragmatic, basic how-to's
                      will be useful to both novices and experienced pros. I think the
                      workbook approach is excellent. Don't call me (on deadline) to ask
                      how to write a press release, -- read Dan's book!" said Peggy Watt,
                      Software News Editor of InfoWorld.

Book helps   "I wrote the book to help small companies present a professional image
small   to the press. Many of these companies who have good products can't
companies   afford to hire a PR firm and consequently, they miss their chance to
                      stand out," said Janal, who introduced the world to CD-ROM technology
                      with Grolier's Electronic Encyclopedia.

Author's   He is president of Janal Communications, a public relations agency
background   specializing in PC hardware and software in Fort Lee, NJ. He chairs the
                      Software Publishers Association's Public Relations Special Interest Group
                      and its PR Boot Camps. He also conducts in-house educational seminars
                      and workshops on public relations, sales and management topics.
                      Formerly an award-winning daily newspaper reporter and editor for eight
                      years, Janal has also written for Computer Dealer, Compute! CompuServe
                      Magazine, Home Office Computing and InfoWorld.

-30-

News Release

For Immediate Release
Contact:
Melissa Haeberlin
Marketing Coordinator
502-491-1900

Inside 1-2-3 Release 3
16-page monthly journal
Editor-in-Chief: Mark A. Kimbell
Price: $69/yr.
Available: October 1990

THE COBB GROUP ANNOUNCES

Inside 1-2-3 Release 3

a monthly "how-to" newsletter for spreadsheet users

Louisville, KY, November 14, 1990—The Cobb Group announces *Inside 1-2-3 Release 3*, a 16-page monthly newsletter providing tips and techniques exclusively for Lotus® 1-2-3® Release 3 and 3.1 users. *Inside 1-2-3 Release 3* is $69 a year for 12 issues.

Contents

Upcoming articles will feature traps and workarounds, database and file management tips, and discussions of new functions and commands. Readers will also receive graphing and printing tips as well as macros and spreadsheet techniques.

"*Inside 1-2-3 Release 3* will help readers navigate more easily through the complex three-dimensional spreadsheet environment of 1-2-3 Release 3 and 3.1. Subscribers will benefit by learning how to use advanced features in easy to read articles with step-by-step instructions," says Mark A. Kimbell, Editor-in-Chief. (Kimbell is also Editor-in-Chief of The Cobb Group's *1-2-3 User's Journal*, which covers Lotus 1-2-3, up to version 2.2.)

Subscribers are encouraged to submit their questions, to provide feedback on the newsletter, and to share their spreadsheet tips with other readers.

Free Issue

A complimentary copy of *Inside 1-2-3 Release 3* is available to anyone who calls 502-491-1900 or 1-800-223-8720.

The Publisher

The Cobb Group is the country's largest publisher of software-specific newsletters. Cobb Group publications support business applications, including spreadsheets, word processors, and databases, as well as operating systems and programming languages.

###

Recycled Paper

General Information, Inc.
11715 North Creek Parkway South, Suite 106
Bothell, Washington 98011
Telephone:(206)483-4555 Fax:(206)485-0666

The Electronic Directory Company

Hot Line Software
Hot Line Directories
The National Directory of Addresses
and Telephone Numbers

NEWS RELEASE

Release on Receipt

For Further Information:
Penny Standal, Jon Austin
206/483-4555

General Information Unveils Toll-Free 800 Edition of HotLine; New Product Brings AT&T's Toll-Free Directory to PCs

BOTHELL, WA – September 24 – General Information, developer of high quality PC-based electronic directory products, today unveiled the latest addition to its product line, the Toll-Free 800 Edition of HotLine, a combination of AT&T's directory of "1-800" toll-free numbers and General Information's award-winning HotLine software.

Designed for small businesses and the office administration market, Toll-Free HotLine fills the need for instant access to important toll-free phone numbers and controlling the costs of long-distance calling and directory assistance.

"The future is shaped by today's innovations," said GI president Joel Horn. "AT&T has been a source of support in the development of a milestone product in the electronic directory industry."

Toll-Free HotLine retails for $59.95, and includes more than 115,000 listings, drawn from AT&T's roster of 1-800 customers. Each listing includes company name, phone number, calling area (nationwide, in-state, etc.) and demographic information such as type of business, usage and more. Users can install the entire file or choose from broad categories and specific business types.

Toll-Free HotLine contains the latest release of GI's very successful HotLine software, featuring a fast, easy-to-use database manager and one of the most powerful and flexible auto dialers available for the PC market. HotLine can be run in a RAM-resident mode (making it available at a keystroke) or as a stand-alone application. HotLine users can create additional directories, add, edit or delete listings and create customized specialty directories. A full-featured notepad and an enhanced utilities package are also part of the latest improvements to HotLine.

Toll-Free HotLine is available directly from General Information and local software retailers. Sales and product information is available by calling 1-800-882-3900.

General Information produces a family of HotLine products that combine directory data for specific markets and geographic areas with enabling software. Additionally, General Information publishes a print product, *The National Directory of Addresses and Telephone Numbers*, that is the largest subscription national directory in the U.S.

#####

Press Release Worksheet

Because many products deserve coverage and reporters are continually under deadline pressure, some press releases that don't contain all the facts are tossed into the garbage. Answer these questions and you will have the makings of a grade-A press release:

1. What is the product name and version number?

    _____

2. What does the product do?

    _____

3. What makes it unique?

    _____

4. How does it differ from competitors?

    _____

5. Who will use the product?

    _____

6. How much does it cost?

    _____

7. (For marketing magazines) How will the product be marketed?

    _____

8. What computer system does it operate under?

    _____

9. What are the product requirements (operating system, memory, graphics, other requirements)?

    _____

10. When will it be available?

    _____

11. Quote a current user on how he or she uses the product.

_____

12. Quote a company official on the usefulness of the product.

_____

13. What is the company's background? (See your company
    positioning statement.)

_____

The final paragraph provides the company's background, position statement, product line and any interesting facts. For instance:

> ECA C&C Products is the United States marketing division of Taiwanese manufacturing giant Chihoo Industries, a major producer of electronics equipment. ECA distributes a full range of scanning products for IBM PC compatible computers.

You now have the basis for writing most press releases logically and clearly. Exceptions will occur as company politicians dictate the placement of certain elements. However, if you answer these questions, reporters can gather the information needed to write an accurate story.

Writing: In House or Agency?

Ken Comdahl, president and chief programmer of a one-person software company, SoftCare Systems, called a public relations agency to revise a press release he had written to announce his new product, Zeamon.

The release lacked a few of the essentials to make it look like a press release, including the dateline and a headline. It contained a few cryptic passages. Nevertheless, the release had a lot of good information. After a few questions and comments, he took another stab at the release. After one more pass, he smoothed out the rough edges and had a professional press release.

He mailed it to editors on a press mailing list he purchased. Two weeks later, reviewers from PC, PC World and PC Computing called him for review copies!

This anecdote proves that programmers can write their own press releases, with a little professional help.

Even though this book will help you write a good press release, you might want to raise your press release to an even more professional level by letting a seasoned writer review the material. You might want to hire a professional writer or public relations agency or a freelancer if:

TIP Fill in the press release worksheet before you give the writing assignment to your agency.

- You've never seen a press release.
- English is not your native language.
- Your grammar is weak.
- You lack design skills.
- You cannot devote the time to write it.

By farming out the press release the first time around and asking a lot of questions, you might pick up tips that will allow you to do it all the next time around. You probably will want to maintain an ongoing relationship with a public relations agency or a free-lance writer so you can get help when you need it.

Since you, the client, have final approval, you're assured the press release will make the right points.

How to Announce a Product Upgrade

If you are announcing an upgrade to your product, that's news. You should write a press release that announces the new features and benefits.

Here is an example of a product upgrade press release. Please read it. Then we will analyze it so you can write one for your product.

MacProof 3.0 Upgrade Works with MacWrite II

SALT LAKE CITY — March 10, 1990 — The newest version of MacProof, version 3.0, allows users of the popular MacWrite II word processor to check the documents for style, grammar, punctuation and usage.

Current MacProof users can get the upgrade for $25 by sending the front page of the manual to the publisher, Lexpertise Linguistic Software, 801 Ninth Avenue, Salt Lake City, UT 00000. The program costs $195 and operates on any Macintosh.

(the press release continues).

The headline tells what is new in seven words. The dateline shows where the company is located and the date. The first paragraph tells what is new and how users will benefit. The second paragraph explains the procedure to obtain an upgrade. The rest of the press release (not shown) follows the standard format for describing information, as discussed in the previous chapter.

When you answer the questions in the following worksheet, you'll have the information you need to write a press release announcing a product upgrade.

Contact: Beverly McDonald
MCI Mail: Alexander Communications
Voice: 404/876-4482
Fax: 404/876-4516

FOR IMMEDIATE RELEASE
August 10, 1990

New Version of Amí, Samna's "Executive"
Word Processor for Windows 3.0 Announced

ATLANTA -- Version 1.2 of Amí, Samna Corporation's "executive" Windows word processor, will begin shipping early September. Compatible with Microsoft Windows 3.0 and Hewlett-Packard's NewWave 3.0, the latest version of Amí, critically acclaimed for its ease-of-use, offers significantly improved performance and a number of powerful new functions.

Designed for the infrequent or casual user, Amí offers the same easy-to-use interface as Amí Professional-Samna's higher-end product. Not as intimidating as character-based word processors, it is ideal for business and education environments where users need to be up and running quickly with a minimal learning curve.

"Amí provides a delicate balance of power and simplicity, meeting the needs of light users at multiple skill levels," explained Samna President and CEO Said Mohammadioun. "The new version offers more capabilities, while maintaining an emphasis on ease-of-use."

Version 1.2 of Amí runs significantly faster under Windows 3.0, and its new features include footnotes; non-printing notes; basic mail-merge capabilities; macro recording and playback; support for DDE (Dynamic Data Exchange) protocols; an enhanced set of import/export filters for text, graphics and data; the ability to anchor frames (to fix the position of text and graphics); more page numbering controls; leader dot tabs; and additional display preferences. Amí version 1.2 also includes new documentation.

-more-

SAMNA CORPORATION • 5600 GLENRIDGE DRIVE • ATLANTA, GEORGIA 30342 • (404) 851-0007

"Since the release of version 1.0, Samna engineers have spent thousands of hours fine-tuning Amí's performance," Mohammadioun stated. "Every area of the program has been examined and improved."

Some of the new enhancements, such as automatic footnotes and non-printing notes, work just as they do in Amí Professional. Other features, such as the basic mail merge and macro capabilities, are subsets of the functions in Amí Professional. For example, macros can be recorded and played in Amí, but cannot be edited as they can in Amí Professional. Amí's mail merge is also designed for simple requirements; it does not provide for advanced or time-intensive tasks that do not fit the profile of an "executive" user, such as conditional merging or label printing.

Version 1.2 of Amí is completely file-compatible with version 1.2 of Amí Professional. Amí can read and edit text in Amí Professional documents, as well as display features not supported in Amí, such as charts and tables. All Amí documents can be read and edited by Amí Professional.

Amí version 1.2 retails for $199 ; registered users of the previous version may upgrade for $49.95.

Amí requires a 286 or higher PC or PS/2 compatibie personal computer; Hercules, CGA, EGA or higher resolution graphics adapter; at least 640K of memory; one floppy drive; one hard disk; DOS 3.0 or higher. A run-time version of Windows 2.11 is available by request, but installation of the full version of Windows 3.0 is recommended.

Founded in 1982, Atlanta-based Samna Corporation is a leading supplier of word processing software and is traded on the NASDAQ stock exchange under the trading symbol SMNA. For further information, contact Samna Corporation, 5600 Glenridge Drive, Atlanta, GA 30342; 404/851-0007.

# # #

news

CONTACT:

Susan Osberg
Lexpertise Linguistic Software
801-359-0059
801-359-0189 (Fax)

LEXPERTISE ANNOUNCES FREE
UPGRADE FOR REGISTERED OWNERS OF
MACPROOF

Las Vegas, Nevada—November 12, 1990—Lexpertise Linguistic Software announced today the release of MacProof 3.2.3. This newest release is now compatible with Quark XPress 3.0, has been enhanced with a new MultiFinder interface, and works with the Macintosh SE, Classic, Mac LC, Mac II, cx, ci, si and fx. Lexpertise is working closely with WordPerfect to assure compatibility with their soon to be released WordPerfect 2.0 for the Macintosh.

Lexpertise will be demonstrating MacProof 3.2.3 in **Merisel's booth #1916 in the Las Vegas Convention Center North Hall**.

MacProof functions as a desk accessory to proofread documents for potential mistakes in writing style and word usage within the word processor or desktop publishing program. Unique to MacProof is a feature which allows user modifications to the usage and spelling dictionaries to create customized checks. MacProof's structural analysis features show text in several different ways, allowing the writer to scan for run-on sentences, sentence fragments and agreement problems.

380 SOUTH STATE STREET

SUITE 202

SALT LAKE CITY

UTAH 84111

TEL 801/359-0059

FAX 801/359-0189

- more -

"Prior to this interim release of MacProof, Quark XPress and WordPerfect users have not had an interactive solution to their proofreading and spell checking needs. This update to MacProof represents Lexpertise's ongoing commitment to making MacProof more accessible to anyone who uses a word processor or desktop publishing program," said Marie Eastman, General Manager of Lexpertise Linguistic Software.

MacProof owners will be updated free of charge if they have sent in the product registration card located inside of the MacProof package. For more information on how to receive the MacProof upgrade, call 1-800-354-5656.

MacProof is also format compatible with MacWrite 4.6 and 5.0, MacWrite II, Microsoft Word 4.0, MindWrite 1.0 and 2.0 and PageMaker 3.0, 3.01, and 3.02 (2MB of memory is required for PageMaker only.) MacProof requires 1 MB RAM and runs on the Macintosh SE, Classic, Mac LC, Mac II, cx, ci, si, and fx.

Lexpertise Linguistic Software, SA, is a leader in text revision, grammar checking and proofreading software. The company was founded in June 1988 in Switzerland. Lexpertise also publishes Bilingual MacProof French, German and Spanish versions as well as PC Proof, Bilingual PC Proof French, German and Spanish versions. All of Lexpertise's products are full featured grammar checkers, style checkers and text revision programs.

Editors may call or write Susan Osberg at 380 South State Street, Suite 202, Salt Lake City, Utah 84111, 801-359-0059 for review copies and screen shots.

-30-

Upgrade Press Release Worksheet

1. What is the product name and version number?

   _____

2. What is the major enhancement?

   _____

3. How will this help the customer?

   _____

4. When will it be available?

   _____

5. What are the other features and benefits of the upgrade?

   _____

   _____

   _____

   _____

   _____

   _____

   _____

Select the top five features that have changed so the press can focus on the importance of the upgrade immediately. Write how these features benefit users. If you can't think of the benefit of a feature, then the feature isn't worth telling a reporter.

Feature	Benefit
1	
2	
3	
4	
5	

6. How does it differ from competitors?

7. Who will use the product?

8. How much does it cost?

9. How can current users get the upgrade?

10. How much will it cost current users to upgrade?

11. (For marketing magazines) How will the product be marketed?

12. What computer system does it operate under?

_____

13. What are the system requirements (operating system, memory,
    graphics, other requirements)?

_____

14. Quote a current user on how he/she likes the product.

_____

15. Quote a company official on the usefulness of the product.

_____

16. What is the background of the company? (See your company
    positioning statement.)

_____

By answering these questions, you have the information you need to write a press
release announcing a product upgrade.

Not every upgrade is worth a separate release. Sometimes a personal note or a
phone call will do. For instance, ECA's color scanner initially did not read the
popular TIF and PCX file formats. Several reviewers said they would not review
the product because it lacked these features. The development team quickly wrote
those features into the program. Here's a letter that explains the update.

May 27, 1990

Mr. Daniel Tynan
PC World Magazine
501 Second Street
San Francisco, CA 94107

Dear Mr. Tynan:

Recently Frank Tzeng of ECA Computer and Communications Products
visited your offices and demonstrated the HICO A4 Color Scanner.

Based on your recommendations, the programmers have added the ability to
read and write files to the TIF and PCX formats. The scanner is now
compatible with the most popular file formats and files can be imported into
all the major desktop publishing programs.

We are in the process of sending new disks to all our registered users.

You will find a copy of the upgraded software in this kit. Please call me if
you have any questions.

Sincerely yours,

Daniel S. Janal
President

ENCLOSURE

DSJ/rrr

Comparison Charts

No product or service is an island. Every product and service has competition. When you are competing, the press needs to see the difference. You can make their jobs easier by creating a chart showing these contrasts.

The chart is a simple grid with your productor service and the competition listed across the top. Features are printed down the side. Put a Y or N in the boxes to designate these features.

The beauty of this chart is that you can control the game. You decide which features to compare and in which order. You can make your product look better in comparison by using a well crafted grid.

When Atari introduced its Atari ST computer, they positioned it against Commodore's Amiga, widely regarded at the time as a breakthrough machine in terms of graphics and sound. Atari created a grid for their press kits and advertisements. The grid noted that the Atari could produce 1024 colors. In the Amiga column, the chart merely said "yes." What the chart failed to say was that the Amiga could produce more than 10 times as many colors as the Atari. Clever, huh?

Moral: He who writes the rules, owns the game.

We urge you to play fair. The press will prove you a liar if you falsify information.

Sample Comparison Chart

	Our product	Brand X	Brand Y
Feature #1	Yes	Yes	No
Feature #2	Yes	No	No
Feature #3	Yes	No	Yes
Feature #4	Yes	Yes	Yes

When Comparing Accounting Capabilities, Great Plains Software Really Checks Out on UNIX

	GPAS	Data Pro	MAS 90	RealWorld	Open Sys	FourGen	CYMA	Solomon	SBT
GL	✓	✓	✓	✓	✓	✓	✓	✓	✓
AR	✓	✓	✓	✓	✓	✓	✓	✓	✓
AP	✓	✓	✓	✓	✓	✓	✓	✓	✓
PR	✓	✓	✓	✓	✓	✓	✓	✓	✓
CM	✓	NO	NO	NO	NO	NO	NO	NO	NO
Bank Rec	✓	✓	✓	✓	NO	NO	NO	NO	NO
OE	✓	✓	✓	✓	✓	✓	✓	✓	✓
IV	✓	✓	✓	✓	✓	✓	✓	✓	✓
PO	✓	✓	✓	✓	✓	✓	✓	✓	✓
JC	✓	✓	✓	✓	✓	NO	✓	✓	✓
IM	✓	✓	✓	NO	NO	NO	NO	✓	NO
RW	✓	✓	✓	✓	✓	✓	✓	✓	✓
Dev Tools	✓	NO	✓	✓	NO	✓	✓	NO	✓
AT&T	✓	✓	NO	✓	✓	✓	NO	NO	NO
SCO	✓	✓	✓	✓	✓	✓	✓	✓	✓

Capabilities

GL - General Ledger
AR - Accounts Receivable
AP - Accounts Payable
PR - Payroll
CM - Cash Management

Bank Rec - Bank Reconciliation
OE - Order Entry
IV - Inventory
PO - Purchase Order
JC - Job Cost

IM - Import Manager
RW - Report Writer
Dev Tools - Developer Tools
AT&T - AT&T UNIX Version
SCO - SCO UNIX/Xenix Version

GREAT PLAINS SOFTWARE
ACCOUNTING AND BUSINESS MANAGEMENT TOOLS

Avoid Hype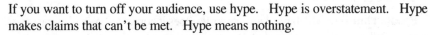

If you want to turn off your audience, use hype. Hype is overstatement. Hype makes claims that can't be met. Hype means nothing.

"The press doesn't need to know that a product is super terrific or any other descriptive words. They need to know what it does," technology writer Stephen Banker said. "All they need to know are the facts."

If you use hype, reporters will chuck away the press release on principle. They know people use these buzzwords because there isn't any hard information in the release. Press releases using buzzwords label the company as an amateur. Avoid these words:

- Next generation
- Revolutionary
- Trend setting
- Rewriting the rules
- One of a kind
- Unique

If your press release says you have a $100 speed-up board that turns an 8088 PC into a 386, the press will wake up and want to look at it. You don't need to hype it. If you tell reporters you have a "one of a kind product" and there is nothing like it, you are waving a red flag in front of them.

"You are challenging us to find another program that does the same thing," said Chris Shipley, executive editor of PC Computing.

Company Backgrounders

If the press is unfamiliar with your company, they might ask to read the company backgrounder. This is text that profiles the company, its objectives and its executives. Written in a narrative style, the company backgrounder can range from 1-20 pages, or more, depending on the company's size. Most small companies will find it best to write about five pages.

The general outline is:

1. **The company and its mission** – What does the company do? What is its long-term objective? How and when was it founded? Where is the company based? Where are branch offices?

2. **Product line** – In which product categories does it compete? What are product names? What do the products do? When were they introduced? Have they won awards?

3. **Executive profiles** – Who are the chairman, president, marketing leaders and design chief? What are their backgrounds? What special skills do they bring to the job?

4. **Financial** – Is the company public or private? For public companies: Where are its shares traded? Who supports this company? How much is the company worth? Which brokers follow the stock? Who is the chief financial officer? What is that person's background? For privately held companies: Who are the financial backers?

5. **Marketing plan** – What are the short-term and long-term marketing goals? How are products distributed? Are co-op plans offered? Other promotional and marketing tactics, both in the United State and abroad.

This outline is general at best. Feel free to adapt the elements to suit your needs. You might want to alter the format if:

- The company was founded by a prominent person
- The company produces other best-selling products
- A major corporation uses your products

Quicksoft Fact Sheet
October 12, 1990

Company: Quicksoft, Inc.
  Founded February 1983. First sales August 1983.

1983 Sales:	$ 17,000.
1984 Sales:	290,000.
1985 Sales:	750,000.
1986 Sales:	1,500,000.
1987 Sales:	1,990,000.
1988 Sales:	1,660,000.
1989 Sales:	2,018,000.

  Privately held.   21 employees (and 1 cat).

President: Bob Wallace
  Born 1949. Founder, Northwest Computer Society, 1976.
  M.S. Computer Science, University of Washington, 1978.
  Employed at Microsoft, 1978-1983 (9th Microsoft employee).
  Product designer/manager, MS-Pascal compiler (IBM Pascal).
  Industry member, past chairman, Washington Software Association.

Vice President:	Megan Dana-Wallace	**Technical**:	8 employees
VP Sales:	Neil Berry	**Operations**:	8 employees
Public Relations:	Terri Downey	**Marketing**:	4 employees

Products: PC-Write Version 3.0, full-featured word processor for the IBM PC.
  Very fast operation, uses standard ASCII text files.
  Friendly, easy to learn and use, help screens, menus.
  Keyboard, screen, printer customization (800+ printers).
  Columns, box moves, automatic reformat, micro-justify.

  PC-Write Lite Version 1.0, simplified word processor.
  Less complex formatting, page preview, Cyrillic support.
  Great for writers, journalists, students, programmers, laptops.

  PC-Browse Version 1.0, pop-up file scan and hypertext tool.
  Finds lost files and information, fast file lookup.
  Easy to create pop-up hypertext information files.

Distribution: Shareware method (one of first users of this method):
  Software diskettes, with all software and instructions, can be
  freely copied and shared by companies, user groups, anybody.

  Quicksoft encourages software users to register for the full price.
  Registered users get current software, complete printed manual,
  phone support and quarterly newsletter for a year, and other
  benefits. Group and Campus licenses available for organizations.

  Shareware Advantages:
  - People can evaluate (and use) software with little risk.
  - Users can get full support and manual with registration.
  - Quicksoft gets promotion and distribution at little cost.
  - Copying and sharing encouraged; no "copying problem".

  International distribution in Germany, France, England, Australia,
  and other countries is handled by our publishing partners in these
  countries. They decide whether to use the shareware approach.

Units sold: 240,700 (52,900 registrations, 94,600 diskettes, 93,200 manuals).

219 First Ave N. #224 · Seattle, WA 98109 · (206) 282-0452

CORPORATE PROFILE
August 1990

Headquarters:	5600 Glenridge Drive Atlanta, Georgia 30342 404/851-0007
Ownership:	Publicly-held; traded on the NASDAQ Stock Exchange under the trading symbol SMNA
Executive Officers:	Said Mohammadioun, Chairman of the Board, President and Chief Executive Officer Bruce Cummings, Executive Vice President of Sales and Marketing John Throckmorton, Vice President of Finance and Corporate Treasurer Robert McKnight, Vice President of National Sales
Founded:	1982
Charter:	Develop and market word processing software programs for all standard business operating systems: PC and MS-DOS, graphics-based environments such as Microsoft® Windows, Hewlett Packard NewWave and the AT&T UNIX®and SCO™ XENIX® operating systems.
Employees:	120
Markets:	The microcomputer spectrum-from small businesses seeking high-quality word processing systems to Fortune 1000 companies, government agencies and legal firms.
Products:	Amí Professional,® Amí,® Samna WORD IV,™ and Samna PLUS IV.™
Support:	Full-time staff of technical support personnel dedicated to manufacturers, resellers, consultants and end users.
Distribution:	Worldwide through Samna's direct sales force, Samna subsidiaries and an international network of dealers, distributors, retailers, value added resellers and systems integrators. Amí is distributed in the U.S. by Ingram Micro D, Softsel, Kenfil and Tech Data; in Canada by Softsel Canada.
Press Contact:	Bevery McDonald, Alexander Communications; 404/876-4482

J&R COMPUTER WORLD FACT SHEET

HOURS:

o 9:00 a.m. – 6:30 p.m. Monday – Saturday
o 10:00 a.m. – 5:00 p.m. Sunday

SERVICES:

o Free analysis and consultation with highly trained sales
  professionals.

o In-store installation and maintenance by factory-trained
  and certified technicians.

MAIL ORDER:

o Convenient telephone ordering: 1-800-221-8180; in New York
  City, 718-417-3737.

SPECIALTY AREAS:

o Corporate Showroom for networking and multi-station
  applications.

o Home Office Center with the latest office equipment,
  word processors and telecommunications products.

o Software Gallery featuring over 5,000 titles and the
  latest computer publications.

o Forty (40) modular PC workstations for hands-on
  demonstration.

BRANDS:

Amdek	Epson	Magnavox	Princeton
Amiga	Everex	Maxell	Samsung
Amstrad	Fuji	Mitsubishi	Sanyo
A.S.T.	Hayes	NEC	Sharp
Atari	Headstart	Novell	Sony
Brother	Hercules	Okidata	Star Micronix
Canon	Hitachi	Osicom	Toshiba
Casio	Intel	Packard-Bell	Vendex
Commodore	Kodak	Panasonic	Video Technologies
Emerson	Leading Tech	Premier	Zenith

(partial listing)

Company Backgrounder Worksheet

1. Applications.   How is the product used? How do different markets use it?

2. Awards, testimonials, prizes.

3. Distribution information. Which distributors carry the product? How is it being marketed? Where are sales offices located?

4. History.   How was the product created? When was it introduced? What is special?

5. Programmers, design team (computer software only). Who created the program? What are their backgrounds.   Have they designed other well-known programs?

The company backgrounder is the first and perhaps only, information the writer has. A good backgrounder will help writers understand what the company stands for, what kinds of products it markets, the quality of management and its financial and marketing muscle.   Done well, a company backgrounder will enhance the article the reporter writes. Done poorly, it might dissuade the reporter from writing about the company.

Case Histories

Case histories are articles showing how your product or service is used. Editors like to print case histories because they are interesting and can be run anytime - a boon to editorial budgets. You can also use case histories as a great backup piece in a press kit. These stories also can be pitched to editors after the new product launch to build momentum. A good case study can put flesh on a product so that the reporter and the ultimate market can understand the full dimensions of how the product or service is used in the marketplace.

Follow this outline to create a good case history:

- Describe the customer's problem. Include a quote.

- The customer used our company's product or service.

- Here's what happened.

- Here's what the user plans to do in the future.

- Quote showing this program helps anyone with similar problems.

Articles range from two paragraphs to five pages, although two pages is a good length to shoot for. Some specialized magazines might print case histories word-for-word. Others rework the material or call the source so they can write an original story or include the material in a roundup article.

If you want to place a case history, use this approach:

- Call the editor, explain the concept, ask for interest (either you write the story or they assign it to their reporter).

- Send an outline of the story.

- Get the assignment confirmed. Nail down the logistics (story length, type of art needed, deadlines for story and art, writing style).

- Write the article, gain approval from customer, send to magazine, arrange for picture to accompany article.

You must promise exclusivity to the magazine in its topic area because editors dislike seeing the same story in their competitors' magazines. You can, however, pitch the story to another magazine in a different industry.

Get Publicity with General Readers

One product can provide different benefits to different users. You therefore must create different pitches to editors of different types of publications. To do this effectively, you must know:

- Who uses your product.
- What information that media needs.

To illustrate: When Grolier introduced its Electronic Encyclopedia, the first software issued on CD-ROM, each reporter was interested in a different story.

- *InfoWorld* wanted to know how the product benefitted users.
- *Computer and Software News* wanted to know the marketing strategy for dealers.
- *Business Week* wanted to know how sales would affect the profitability of the parent company.
- *Popular Science* wanted to know how the new technology worked.
- *Classroom Computer Learning* wanted the names of teachers who used the product.

Each editorial audience wanted the answers to a different set of questions. As the PR person, you are required to think as each reporter would and provide the best possible answer that tells your company story and meets the reporters' needs.

If you do this, your product can get coverage in a variety of publications beyond the traditional computer press.

Let's do a few exercises that will help you create messages for different audiences. Let's look at Hotline, an auto dialer software program. The first market is anyone who uses a computer and makes a lot of phone calls. The second market is professional telemarketers and sales people who make many calls and need to take notes. The third could be school truant officers who call parents. Get the idea? It is easy. If you have any problems, talk to the marketing and sales staff and ask how the product is being used. Chances are good that a vertical market publication interested in your story. The worksheet on the following pages will help you determine the message for a non-technology audience.

Vertical Market Worksheet

1. What is the audience for your product? What can they do with it?

    _____

    _____

2. Which magazines cover this market?

    _____

    _____

3. Who else can use the product? What can they do with it?

    _____

    _____

4. Which magazines cover this market?

    _____

    _____

5. What is a third audience for your product?

    _____

    _____

6. Which magazines cover this market?

    _____

    _____

Now you determine what you want to tell each reporter in the media that covers those markets. Reporters must answer several key questions for their readers.

These questions are:

1. How will my readers benefit from this?

    _____

    _____

2. What does the product do?

_____

_____

3. How much does it cost?

_____

_____

4. What computer system does it require?

_____

_____

5. What are the system requirements (operating system, memory, graphics, other requirements)?

_____

_____

6. What is the background of the company?

_____

_____

7. Quote a current user on how he/she likes the product.

_____

_____

8. Quote a company official on the usefulness of the product.

_____

_____

Ensure Reviewers See Prime Benefits

How can you ensure that a reviewer notices your product's outstanding features?

You can leave it to chance and hope they will find the new feature, or you can take matters into your own hands. How can you expect reviewers to find new features located three menus deep?

To make sure the highlights are covered, create "Reviewers Guidelines" a one-page tip sheet filled with program highlights and comparisons to competing products.

The following illustration presents a copy of a pitch letter to reviewers who requested copies of MacProof. Notice how it subtly tells reviewers what is new, how it compares and what they should look for.

TIP

Create positioning statements for each major feature.

Although this sample is incorporated into a letter to convey a friendly, businesslike tone, you could also create a separate sheet that has a heading "Reviewers Guidelines" and presents the same content.

Another format is the storyboard. The Learning Company uses this approach to get the point across quickly and colorfully for their Super Solvers Midnight Rescue. A "quick hints " format illustrated in their notepad for Super Solvers Challenge of the Ancient Empires.

The Learning Company

6493 Kaiser Drive
Fremont, CA 94555

☎ 1-800-852-2255

Super Solvers™
Midnight Rescue!™

A *Next Generation* Children's Software Title!

Captivating New Program Combines Exciting
Arcade-Action With Rich Educational Benefits

CAN YOU READ, THINK, AND REACT IN TIME TO RESCUE THE SCHOOL BEFORE IT DISAPPEARS?

Morty Maxwell, the Master of Mischief, has taken over Shady Glen School! Disguised as one of his five robots, he and his team are painting the entire school with disappearing paint. As a Super Solvers Club Member, you must find out which robot is the Master of Mischief. But you only have until midnight in this fast-action adventure to explore the school, read for clues, and collect facts to out-think your clever opponent. Accumulate enough points to reach the rank of Champion and you can give the Master a taste of his own Mischief!

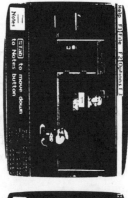

Explore the hallways and rooms. Look for special signs to read for clues that will help you find the Master of Mischief.

Be quick! You'll have to think and move fast to avoid tricks that the camera shy robots will throw at you.

Track down the robots and take their pictures with your magic camera. You'll capture important facts!

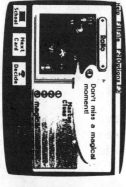

Go to your notes to compare your reading clues and your robot pictures to deduce which robot is the Master of Mischief!

COUNCIL WANTS SUPER SOLVERS

SHADY GLEN, March 16, 1989 -- The Shady Glen City Council voted 7 to 0 yesterday to hire the Super Solvers to help solve the mysteries of the past several months. "There was really no contest," ...

Read carefully for clues that the Master of Mischief has hidden in the posters, newsletters, and books for you to find.

Time is running out . . . be sure of your facts before you make an accusation, or both you and the school will disappear!

The Super Solvers had a record. Their cases were tried and true. Name the kind of things they solved, And that will be your clue.

book
disappearing
freezing
magical

He will later challenge you to see if you can recall what you've read! So, take your time and get it right!

You've won! You have found the Master of Mischief before he made the school disappear! Play again to maximize your points and move up in rank!

The Game Plan

- **Look for artifact pieces** scattered in the chambers and collect them. You'll find enough pieces in each chamber to assemble one artifact.
- **Study the layout of the chambers** and learn how the panels and conveyor belts that block your way operate. Take your time to figure things out.
- **Use your tools** to overcome obstacles and protect yourself from cave creatures and flying objects that rob you of energy.
- **Watch your energy meter.** When you get low, be on the lookout for energy apples to restore your energy. For a full supply of energy, solve the logic problem on the first try.
- **Find the passageway** out of each chamber by collecting all the artifact pieces and arranging them in the right order on your puzzle table.
- **Solve the logic problem** in the passageway to unlock the door and get out of the chamber.
- **Successfully explore the first four caverns** and then you can go on to the fifth cavern, the Ancient World, which leads to the ultimate challenge of the ancient empires!

Date

Name
Title
Publication
Address
City, State ZIP

Dear NAME,

I enjoyed meeting you at Macworld.   Thank you for your interest in reviewing MacProof from Lexpertise Linguistic Software.   The review software and press kit are enclosed in this package.

As you review the program please note:

- MacProof is the only desk accessory grammar checker for the Macintosh, which means consumers can interactively edit and update their documents. Other programs require you to close the file, exit the word processing program and load their program and select the file —a long and tedious process.

- MacProof retains the formatting characteristics of PageMaker, so consumers can add a spelling checker to PageMaker.

- MacProof has text revision tools, in addition to grammar and style checking.   This means consumers can raise their writing to a higher level. It is like having an English teacher look over your shoulder and remind you to check sentence beginnings for redundancy. It also offers a visual way to check for transitions and logic.

- MacProof 3.2.1, released in January, works with MacWrite II, the most popular word processing program.

- MacProof is the oldest updated grammar checker for the Macintosh, so consumers can be assured of using a time-tested program.

Please call me if you have any questions or if you need screen shots.   For technical support, call Sue Osberg at 801-xxx-xxxx.

Sincerely yours,

Daniel S. Janal
President

ENCLOSURE
DSJ/rrr

Reviewer's Guidelines

As you review the program please note:

■ MacProof is the only desk accessory grammar checker for the Macintosh, which means consumers can interactively edit and update their documents. Other programs require you to close the file, exit the word processing program and load their program and select the file — a long and tedious process.

■ MacProof retains the formatting characteristics of PageMaker, so consumers can add a spelling checker to Pagemaker.

■ MacProof has text revision tools in addition to grammar and style checking. This means consumers can raise their writing to a higher level. It is like having an English teacher look over your shoulder and remind you to check sentence beginnings for redundancy. It also offers you a visual way to check for transitions and logic.

■ MacProof is the oldest updated grammar checker for the Macintosh, so consumers can be assured of using a time-tested program.

Please call me if you have any questions or if you need screen shots. For technical support, call Sue Osberg at 801-xxx-xxxx.

Another format is the guided tour. This is a demo with step-by-step instructions, complete with keystrokes, diagrams and screen shots. It will take time to produce this road map, but it is worthwhile because the reviewer will see the highlighted features. Notice how this is done with a story board format used by The Learning Company on the following page.

Reasons to Review Sheets ■

Want to get reporters to sit up and take notice of your products? Create a "Reasons to Review" sheet. This printed document provides a one-paragraph description of the product, another paragraph on its benefits and as many applications as you can think of. These applications show the different ways the product can be used to solve problems. In the illustration on the next page provided by Technopolis Communications, nine reasons are given to entice reviewers to take notice.

The release also provides the system requirements and ordering information in the body copy. This give the publicist the flexibility of sending the sheet to reporters either with the press kit or with a cover letter. Notice the unique layout on the left column that provides a routing slip, editorial contact and company contact.

Question and Answer Sheets

When the technology you are introducing is new, a Question and Answer Sheet can help you tell your message effectively. You would also write a press release announcing the product. The press release would talk briefly about the new technology. The Q and A Sheet helps clarify the technology and gives more background than is necessary in a press release.

Q and A Sheets can also be used to clarify controversies, investor relations material and other matters that would be too lengthy to cover in a press release.

To prepare a good Q and A Sheet, you must think like a reporter. What questions would a reporter ask? Those are the questions you should answer. A good way to think of questions is to have a brainstorming session with your marketing department. Better yet, call reporters you know well and tell them the product's positioning statement and benefits. Write down their questions. If they have questions, chances are other reporters will have the same questions. Answer them in the Q and A Sheet.

A sample Q and A Sheet for Samna is shown following the "Resons to Review" example.

Dariana Technology Group Inc.

REASONS TO REVIEW SYSTEM SLEUTH 2.0

Diagnostic software knows what lurks inside personal computers, turns users into gumshoes able to solve hardware-software conflicts, map PC configuration without screwdriver

Product description

System Sleuth 2.0 comprises a battery of diagnostic software tests and comprehensive reports designed to help users compile information about, troubleshoot, and optimally configure a personal computer.

Product benefits

System Sleuth 2.0 eliminates hours of frustrating trial and error. Users are no longer forced to open the computer, painstakingly disassembling and reconstructing it one component at a time, just to see what's going on under the hood and behind the screen.

Applications

❶ Holster that smoking screwdriver! Unravel configuration puzzles, delve into the dark secrets of hammerlocked terminate-and-stay-resident programs (TSRs), cross-examine memory, interrogate hard disks, probe display mysteries, and dig for hardware and software clues -- *without opening up the computer.*

❷ Are you often called on to help set up or fix computers for other users? System Sleuth 2.0 displays a "System Overview" that gives you the information you need about what's in the system. Then pull down the "I/O Card" submenu for the locations of expansion cards -- and where to install new components.

❸ How true is your clone? System Sleuth 2.0 identifies your ROM BIOS by copyright and date, determines which central processor and math coprocessor, if any, is installed, and which version of DOS is actually running.

❹ Are your TSRs fighting over the same RAM? System Sleuth 2.0 maps the TSRs, applications programs and device drivers running in base, extended and expanded memory, including your mouse and memory manager, if active.

❺ Just how sharp is that display? System Sleuth 2.0 tests the display adapter and monitor and lists the video modes supported and the amount of video memory.

❻ Where has all that data gone? System Sleuth 2.0 investigates the partition tables, low-level details, file sectors, disk statistics and bad sectors of a hard disk.

Attention:

☐ Software editors
☐ Utility editors
☐ Review editors
☐ Computer editors
☐ Business editors
☐ New product editors

Editors contact:

Steven J. Leon
Technopolis™ Communications
6000 Canterbury Dr. D301
Culver City, Calif. 90230
✆ 213-670-5606
(FAX) 213-670-2064

Company contact:

Frank Westall
Director
Dariana Technology Group Inc.
7439 La Palma Ave. #278
Buena Park, Calif. 90620-2698
✆ 714-994-7400
(FAX) 714-994-7401

(more)

⊘ Got a bad chip and an indecipherable error message? System Sleuth 2.0 ferrets out malfunctions for replacement.

⊘ Do you have a special-purpose component with a custom-programmed diagnostic utility? System Sleuth 2.0 may be used as DOS "shell." It's an open platform. You can add in -- *and run* -- other diagnostics, even other application programs.

⊘ Take inventory! System Sleuth 2.0 prints comprehensive reports that document the entire system or any component. Also, network administrators and service and support personnel can use the comprehensive reporting functions to generate "snapshots" of systems on a network and in use at an organization or in a department, creating a system inventory for reference and troubleshooting.

System requirements

System Sleuth 2.0 requires an IBM PC, XT, AT, PS 2 or compatible, 256K RAM, and MS/PC-DOS 2.1 or PC-MOS/386 version 2.1 or higher. The program supports monochrome, Hercules, CGA, EGA and VGA displays.

Ordering information

System Sleuth 2.0 retails for $149.95. Users of System Sleuth 1.0 may upgrade for $35.00.

The program is distributed by Softsel Computer Products and is on the shelves of major retail chains such as Egghead and Software City.

System Sleuth 2.0 may be ordered from Dariana Technology Group Inc., 7439 La Palma Ave. #278, Buena Park, Calif. 90620-2698, ☏ 714-994-7400, (FAX) 714-994-7401 ▉

Editors:

Review copies, black-and-white and color photos are available upon request.

Ami and Ami Professional

Questions & Answers

Q. **What is the concept behind the Amí® and Amí Professional® word processing packages?**

A. Simply stated, Amí and Amí Professional are the fastest, easiest way to get your ideas into a computer and then onto paper as professional-looking documents. And, just as the name suggests -- Amí means "friend" in French -- the packages are very user-friendly. They're both easy-to-learn and easy-to-use. Amí and Amí Professional use the intuitive graphics of the Microsoft® Windows interface to show you everything you need to know to get from concept to final document quickly and efficiently.

Q. **Why are Amí and Amí Professional based on Microsoft Windows?**

A. Microsoft Windows brought the user-friendliness of the Apple Macintosh to the IBM PC platform. One key benefit is that Windows' graphical interface and mouse pointer allow you to take in much more information at a glance than mere text does. Under Windows, you get true WYSIWYG -- what you see is what you get. In Amí and Amí Professional, you can see the results of your format changes instantly on the screen, and you won't get any surprises when you send your document to the printer.

Another advantage of using Windows is that it provides a standard way of working with the screen, one that is consistent across all products that adhere to it. If you have learned how to use one Windows-based software program, it's usually easy to learn how to use another one -- often much easier than it is to move among conventional programs that may have radically different user interfaces.

Q: **Why do you have two word processing packages for Windows?**

A: Amí and Amí Professional were designed to meet the graphical word processing needs of an entire organization -- from casual and executive users to "power users." Ami features all the standard word processing functions, with the main focus on simplicity of operation. Ami Professional retains the same high degree of ease-of-use, while offering a comprehensive range of sophisticated word processing functions and desktop publishing features. Regardless of whether the user is a clerk in the steno pool, a middle manager, an executive secretary or chief executive officer, either Amí or Amí Professional will provide just the right level of sophistication. And because Amí and Amí Professional are complementary products, users of each package can share the same document -- no matter whether it was created in Amí or Amí Professional. This is a particular advantage in offices where both packages are in use in order to fit the requirements of users with differing levels of need and experience. Because they share the same user interface, it's easy for an Amí user to learn how to use the high-end features of Amí Professional.

Q. **What makes Amí and Amí Professional different from other word processors already on the market?**

A. Amí and Amí Professional are radically different from other word processors because they represent the next generation of word processing software -- products that are visually oriented, easy-to-use and capable of producing a wide variety of documents. Instead of using complicated command-key sequences, Amí and Amí Professional have made word processing features much more easily accessible. Pull-down menus, a "what you see is what you get" (WYSIWYG) display and graphic feedback windows take the guesswork out of using the products. Also, by offering a revolutionary implementation of "style sheets," Amí and Amí Professional significantly reduce the amount of time it takes users to go from entering text to producing finished documents.

Increase Publicity with Pictures

Photos increase the likelihood that a publication will write about your product because many publications need artwork to brighten their pages. It is not unusual for one product to be included in a news brief column while a similar product is displayed with a picture in the main news section. The only difference is that a picture was available for one and not the other.

There are three main types of pictures: product shots, screen shots and product box shots. Editors prefer them in two formats: black -and -white prints and color transparency.

Work with a photographer experienced in these types of shoots. Special expertise is required to shoot computer screens to avoid a black, horizontal bar across every screen photograph. There is a filter to reduce or eliminate screen flicker.

When you send photos, attach a sheet of paper that contains a cutline, which identifies the product and explains what is happening in the picture. This information should fit in two sentences. Include the company name, phone number and contact person. Frequently, the picture becomes separated from the press kit when the editor gives the photo to the art department. If you identify the picture, it won't get lost.

Keep adequate supplies of each format in stock so you can send them to reporters at a moment's notice. Art directors usually need the pictures yesterday because of the speed at which daily and weekly newspapers work. If the product has wide appeal, you will need many copies. If the program provides swimming pool technicians with the proper mixture of chemicals, you will need a handful of photos.

TIP

Don't send photos of company executives, as magazines rarely use them

Ideally, you will include at least one photo with every press kit. However, because photos are expensive (about $1 apiece in quantity for black and white) your budget might not allow you to send photos out with 400 press kits. That's okay. Magazines will call you if they want a picture. You can send it to them by overnight courier so they will meet their deadlines. However, you do run the risk of missing opportunities from magazines that simply print photos received and don't need to call for more pictures.

Photos of company executives are rarely used in a product story. Don't waste resources by distributing hundreds of photos. Have a few copies in your files for special occasions.

Examples of screen shots follow.

MONOLOGUE 2.0 GIVES POWER OF SPEECH TO PCs --

Monologue 2.0 from First Byte synthesizes text and data into a clear, smooth, natural-sounding adult male or female voice that users hear through the speaker built into an IBM-or-compatible PC.

Photo 1 is a screen shot that shows the Monologue 2.0 configuration menu. Photo 2 is a screen-shot overview of Monologue 2.0 capabilities. Photo 3 highlights a block of numbers for Monologue 2.0 to convert to synthesized speech.

For information: First Byte, 714-432-1740, or Technopolis, 213-670-5606.

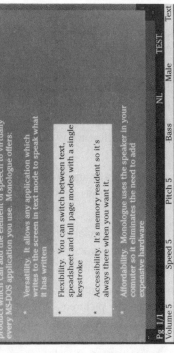

Photo 2

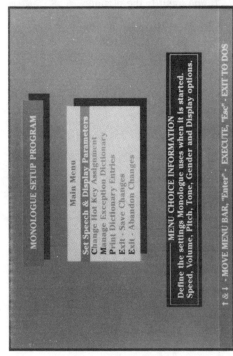

Photo 1

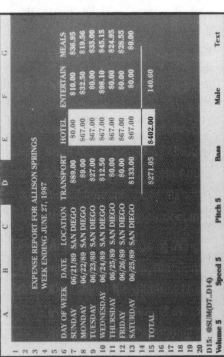

Photo 3

NEW MONITORS FOR IBM AND MAC COMPUTERS FROM NANAO USA CORP. -- The 16-inch FlexScan 9080i, top, and 20-inch FlexScan 9400i, bottom, are flicker-free, high-refresh rate, low VLF radiation, color, multiscanning models. The monitor at the left of each photo shows IBM software and, at the right, Mac software. For information: Nanao USA Corp., 213-325-5202; or Technopolis, 213-670-5606.

Charts, graphs and line art

Charts, graphs and line art can help tell your story to the media. If you are releasing the results of a survey or have other material involving heavy use of numbers, consider adding a chart or graph that tells your story clearly and vividly. Provide camera ready art that editors can print in their publications.

Provoke Interest with Response Cards

Consider enclosing a response card with your release so reporters can ask for review products or more information without even lifting the phone. A response card is a simple postage-paid postcard with your return address on one side. On the flip side is the name of the product, the desired computer format (IBM/Macintosh, disk size) and fill-in lines for the reporter's name, title, publication, phone number and address and projected review date. Additional information and data can reflect your company's needs.

The response card serves another time-saving purpose. You might not have time to call the secondary or tertiary tier press - those reporters you'd like to call if only you had another hand and 10 more hours in the day. Sending a response card to those reporters gives you the opportunity to get information from them and deliver product to them.

Sample Response Card

Yes, please send me a copy of _____ for review purposes. Please send me the product in this format:

__ IBM __ Macintosh__ 3.5 inch disk __ 5.25 inch disk _____ Other

Name_____ Phone _____

Title_____ __ ___

Magazine _____

City_____State _____ Zip _____

Anticipated Review Date_____

    ❑ Please call me to arrange an interview
    ❑ Please send these photos ❑ screen ❑ package ❑ color ❑ BxW
    ❑ I am interested in ❑ case histories ❑ business applications
    ❑ government applications ❑ educational applications

Save Money on Printing

Your materials should look professional, but you needn't waste money paying for glitz. The press doesn't care if your release is printed on 60-pound, colored paper with colored envelopes. They just want useful information.

The most economical, cost-effective press releases are produced on plain 20-pound bond paper with the company's letterhead. Some companies think a colored press release stands out, but that's not the case. A press release should not look like a brochure, pamphlet or any other sales material. Jeff Silverstein, publisher of the Digital Information Group, was not impressed with a stunning press release with big headlines, pictures, lots of color and very little text.

"It doesn't look like it contains the information I am looking for," he said.

If the press release is too fancy, a reporter might think it is a brochure or sales piece that doesn't contain the hard information needed to write the story. Editors dislike receiving publicity material identical to items meant for dealers or distributors.

Because reporters receive so much material every day – including dozens of press releases printed on colored paper – yours won't stand out just because it looks glitzy. Rich Malloy, the executive editor of *ByteWeek,* receives about three feet of press releases each day. And the unsolicited software can be measured in shelves! What stands out, however, are return addresses. The press looks at a return address and thinks:

TIP

Concentrate on content, not glitz.

- "This is a great company. They do good work. I better look at this."

- "This is a company I've never heard of. I'll give it a shot."

- "This is a company that I've seen before. I don't like their product. I'm going to chuck out it without even reading it."

If you develop good products and a good rapport with the press, your releases will get noticed.

Chapter 3 Targeting the Media

Know Your Reporter

Know your reporters. Know what they cover. Know how their magazine positions itself and its audience. You must know which magazines write about your products and what slant they take if you are going to be effective.

Nothing gives the PR industry a worse name than lazy people who call reporters and ask "What do you write about?" or "What does your magazine cover?"

Reporters continually tell publicists to read their publications. Reporters' biggest gripes are the PR people who don't understand what the magazine stands for, who reads it and what they are interested in. This section will concentrate on how to find reporters who are interested in your products.

Find the Right Target

You can create a media list by reading the magazines that cover your products. Every magazine has a masthead that lists editors and provides addresses and phone numbers. This listing will not detail what reporters cover, however. It might list whether they cover hardware or software, or work out of a bureau. To find reporters who cover your area, read magazines and look for bylines. Or call the magazine and ask the news editor or managing editor for the person who covers your area.

To find more detailed information than is printed on the masthead, you can conduct research in any number of directories, which are outlined below. As with any printed data, information can be outdated the minute the book is published. Don't be surprised to find the reporter has switched to a new beat, or has left the magazine. Two major sources of information for the high tech reporting community include:

Media Map. This directory is thorough in its approach to listing the names, phone numbers and specialties of everyone listed on the masthead of business oriented computer magazines, general interest magazines, newspapers, analysts, newsletters and columnists. It also lists editorial calendars, the publication's positioning statement, ad prices, demographics and other items. It costs $1,900 and includes a database of reporters. (Media Map, 130 The Great Road, Bedford, MA 01730, 617-275-5560.)

Bacon's Publicity Checker. The grand daddy of media directories, Bacon's lists thousands of magazines in hundreds of vertical markets, including computer publications. The publicity checker gives media information on 17,000 magazines and newspapers in the US and Canada. It is published annually in October for $160. For an additional $160, you can get editorial calendars for computer and general business press. The Radio/TV Directory ($160) includes over 9,000 radio and 1,300 TV station listings. The International Publicity Checker ($175) lists 11,200 business, trade and industrial publications and more than 1,000 newspapers in 15 countries in Western Europe. On the negative side, it doesn't provide magazine positioning statements or expanded mastheads. (Bacon's Clipping Bureau, 332 S. Michigan Avenue, Chicago, IL, 60604, 1-800-621-0561, 312-922-2400).

Media Distribution Services (307 West 36th Street, New York, NY 10018, 212-279-4800) Maintains a computerized database of virtually every technical, business and consumer publication in the country. They provide complete mailing services, including printing, labeling and mailing the press release.

The following exercises will help you set priorities and determine which editors should get your immediate attention.

Reportorial Triage

On the old television show M★A★S★H, whenever incoming wounded troops flooded the hospital area, the nurses and doctors created a triage unit that sorted the soldiers into categories: those soldiers that were beyond help, those soldiers who could manage on their own and those soldiers they could save. The doctors operated on the ones that seemed most likely to live. The doctors understood the need to devote their most valuable resources to the most likely prospects.

So it is with reporters. All reporters are not created equal. Some magazines are more important than others. Some can help you bring your product to life. Others can't help at all. Because you have a limited amount of time and resources to visit editors, make appointments and send review equipment and software, you should set priorities.

One way to do this is to divide the press into three tiers. The A list consists of the reporters who really matter. The B list is comprised of reporters who you should talk to. The C list includes reporters who are at the periphery of your needs. By setting up this list in advance, you can easily determine which reporters to call first when arranging interviews and demos at a trade show, for example. You will want to spend your energy and money on the A list first and then on the B list as a backup. When you need to fill in the gaps, you can go to the C list.

If your resources are short and you can only send out 25 copies of your product, you will find this A-B-C list very helpful in determining who should get top priority.

To determine where each magazine fits depends on the product you are promoting. Read through one of the references sources or hire a PR specialist or analyst in this area to help you select the key publications. Your advertising agency might be able to help.

Let's create your lists now. Write the name of the publication, reporter who covers the product, phone number and triage rank. This system allows for flexibility. If you have identified 10 A list magazines, that's fine. Every product is different. The important factor is to get you to start doing this mental exercise so you can save time later. This list also will come in handy if you decide to delegate assignments.

Reportorial Triage Worksheet

The key press for my product is:

Computer	Reporter	Telephone	Triage Rank
1			
2			
3			
4			
5			

Business Press

	Reporter	Telephone	Triage Rank
1			
2			
3			
4			
5			

Retail Press

	Reporter	Telephone	Triage Rank
1			
2			
3			
4			
5			

Daily Newspapers

	Reporter	Telephone	Triage Rank
1			
2			
3			
4			
5			

Consumer/General	Reporter	Telephone	Triage Rank
1			
2			
3			
4			
5			

Educational Press			
1			
2			
3			
4			
5			

Syndicated Columnists	Telephone	Triage Rank
1		
2		
3		
4		
5		

Analysts/Opinion Leaders	Telephone	Triage Rank
1		
2		
3		
4		
5		

Once you have the information, you need to manage it. That's the focus of the next chapter.

Keep Track of the Media

Computers can keep track of the names, addresses and phone numbers of reporters who cover your product category. Having this information in a database will help you in a variety of ways. You can print labels, form letters and envelopes as well as telephone directories, progress reports, call back lists, to-do lists and the like.

Creating a database is relatively easy. If you have any degree of computer literacy, you should have the expertise to create and use a database within a few minutes. If you want to create reports, call back sheets and other data manipulation, you might consider using a sales contact program.

You can also maintain your press list with a simple database program, of which there are many good and inexpensive ones. When you create the database include these fields:

> Salutation
> First name
> Last name
> Title
> Publication
> Address 1
> Address 2
> City
> State
> Zip
> Phone
> Fax
> Interests
> System
> Notes
> Products sent

These fields will give you flexibility to create labels, letters and reports. This system should work easily with most word processing or list management software.

Chapter 4 Getting the Word Out

What is News?

Many opportunities exist to publicize your products and services. Here is a brief description of the topic categories and what information qualifies:

News

Just as it implies, this is the basic news story announcing a new service, new product or upgrade to an existing product, surveys, trends, reaction to major news, industry sales figures, industry growth projections, significant contracts, mergers and acquisitions, patents, law suits, company earning figures, initial public offerings, massive hirings and firings and the like. Call the managing editor of small publications. At large publications, separate news editors might be assigned to different topics, such as hardware, software, contracts, systems and the like.

Contract awards

Important contracts of companies and agencies can be covered as news articles. Less significant contracts can be awarded one-paragraph notices. Call the news editor.

Personnel appointments

News and photographs of important personnel changes at significant companies. A touchy subject with many magazines, editors either love personnel announcements or hate them. Check the magazine before sending the release. If they print personnel appointments, they also usually print a head shot.

New literature

Articles on books, periodicals, reports, surveys, studies and the like.

Book reviews

Reviews of books written by staff members or free lance writers.

Signed articles

Opinion pieces by the president or chief engineer or marketer of your company. Topics include current trends, future forecasts or comments on top news items, such as the threat of competition from Japan. Articles cannot be self serving. You can't write about how your company has designed the best mousetrap.

Letters to the editor

These signed letters are great ways to state your opinions. You can either add information to an industry trend story, correct information, or raise an important point your industry should discuss.

Calendar

Notices of upcoming events, such as trade shows, conferences, expositions, seminars, workshops and the like. A calendar editor handles this clerical function. Usually, a paragraph is printed with the time, date, place, market and phone number for information. Major trade shows, such as Comdex, PC Expo and MacWorld can be covered in greater depth. Call the calendar editor or news editor.

Take Advantage of Breaking News

When news breaks in your industry, reporters scurry to find experts who can put the matter in perspective. As an industry insider, you might qualify. Call the editor when you hear of breaking news and discuss how you think the news will affect the industry.

This strategy benefits you in several ways:

- You gain coverage for yourself, company and product. You will be identified by name, title and company - and possibly - company position ing statement. For instance:

  "This ruling spells trouble for the industry because it will put a chilling effect on research and development," said Sarah Scott, vice president of technology for Widget World, of Technology Park, CA, a leading manufacturing of class-A style components.

- You build rapport with the reporter. You have done a favor. Next time news breaks, the reporter will call you.
- You will be seen as an industry leader or expert. After all, the reader thinks you must be important, otherwise the press wouldn't quote you.

Here is a system to make sure this strategy works.

- Identify speakers from your company.
- Discuss the benefits and opportunity for publicity. Some officials might not be familiar with the company's promotional objectives or might be afraid of reporters.

- Send a list of contacts, complete with titles, desk phone numbers and home phone numbers to reporters along with a cover letter explaining that these people would be delighted to comment on the selected topics.
- Create a news monitoring service on CompuServe which alerts you to industry news.
- Check the news monitoring service twice a day (morning and mid-afternoon).
- Call reporters when news breaks.

Possible news comment opportunities include: new services, new products or upgrades to existing products, surveys, trends, industry sales figures, industry growth projections, significant contracts, mergers and acquisitions, patents, law suits, company earning figures, initial public offerings, massive hirings and firings and the like.

If you stay on top of news and make your company accessible, you will build strong relationships with reporters and get publicity.

News Commenting Worksheet

1. Identify speakers from your company, direct dial phone number and home phone number:

	Person	Title	Direct Dial	Home Phone
a. Marketing issues				
b. Technical issues				
c. Financial issues				
d. Legal issues				
e. Other issues (based on your industry needs)				

2. Create a list of daily and weekly news publications covering your industry.

Publication	Reporter	Phone Number

1 _____

2 _____

3 _____

4 _____

5 _____

3. Create a news monitoring service on CompuServe which alerts you to industry news. You will need to create a list of search terms, sometimes called "key words" which identify the topics you want the computer to search such as: computer, hardware, software, high technology, chemicals, biotechnology, or science.

Search terms (key words)

1 _____

2 _____

3 _____

4 _____

Write Pitch Letters That Are Read

Reporters respond favorably to cover letters sent with press releases, especially if the letter relates to their needs. Sending a cover letter, or pitch letter, can increase the chances of a product review. For that reason, we will devote the next few pages to the art of writing pitch letters.

A pitch letter is a one-page correspondence that accompanies your press release or press kit. Its purpose is to entice the reporter to become interested in your product. You have a lot of latitude in writing the pitch letter. You can be creative, witty, entertaining and imaginative. However, don't go overboard.

Peggy Watt, software editor of *InfoWorld*, shared a few pitch letters that went awry. Here are a few themes that crop up:

- Write about my product or I'll lose my job.
- Write about my product or I won't advertise.
- Write about my product because I'm just out of school.

Reporters don't care about your job. They care about keeping their jobs. If you want to help reporters keep their jobs, offer them news, features and other story ideas that are in line with what they write.

Most major publications keep a strict wall between the advertising and editorial departments so the advertising won't influence the editorial integrity of the magazine. By offering a bribe, such as your advertising dollars, you ensure that reporters will not write about your product.

TIP Personalize the pitch letter whenever possible.

Pitch letters should keep the reporter's interests in mind. Freelancer Nat Satkowski, said he reads every pitch letter. If the letter addresses the needs of his audience,, he reads it. The message is clear: know your reporters' interests and tell them how your product can meet their needs to write stories.

Now let's look at a pitch letter that gets the basics across in a factual, informative and friendly basis. The company needed a letter that grabbed their interest and showed that grammar checkers are useful. This example illustrates the three parts to a pitch letter:

- Gain their attention.
- Give them essential facts.
- Get their orders.

After studying the example, you can practice in a worksheet.

Sample Pitch Letter

DATE

Name
Title
Publication
Address
City, State ZIP

Dear Editor:

Before your say "Oh no, not another grammar checker," let's look at how PC Proof from Lexpertise Linguistic Software stands apart from the market.

PC Proof is the first grammar checker that contains revision tools to help writers communicate clearly, concisely and accurately. The enclosed press release describes this process in detail.

PC Proof offers another distinction from Grammatik and RightWriter: native speakers of French or German can use Bilingual PC Proof to catch errors when they write in English.

For instance, in French, the word "chef" means president. Imagine receiving a letter from a French colleague saying he likes your proposal but first must gain the approval of his chef!

I will call you in a few days to answer your questions. Please call me if you would like to receive software for review.

Sincerely yours,

Daniel S. Janal
President

ENCLOSURE
DSJ/rrr

Pitch Letter Worksheet

1. Gain their attention. Write two sentences that will gain attention, or reporters won't read the rest of the letter.

   _____

   _____

   _____

   _____

   _____

   _____

   _____

2. Give reporters essential facts (Remember, you are enclosing the press release or press kit that will round out the highlights you present in the pitch letter).

   _____

   _____

   _____

   _____

3. Ask for the order. Tell them how they can get in touch with you or how you will reach them.

   _____

   _____

   _____

   _____

4. Test the message with a colleague. Or better yet, a friend. If they understand and are interested, you have a winning letter.

Phone Pitching - Making Sure Reporters Take Your Call

Phone pitching is one of the most successful strategies for getting press coverage. In one phone call, you can:

- Convince a reporter to write a news article or review.
- Determine what action the reporter will take.
- Build rapport that will help you in the future.

However, calling reporters can be the hardest part of the PR person's job. Many people dread talking to people they don't know. They also fear the rejection that invariably accompanies many calls. Even experienced PR people feel this way.

To overcome phone fear, follow these steps:

- Fear of reporters. Get to know everything about them.
- Fear of magazine. Learn about the magazine's focus.
- Fear of rejection. Target your audience carefully and target the message. If you give the reporter what he or she needs, you will invariably get what you need.
- Fear of talking. Practice your pitch with a colleague.

The amount of success you will have is tied directly to information. If you know your product, the reporters, their audience and your message, you will greatly enhance your chances of getting your product covered.

Here are a series of guidelines from Beverly MacDonald of Alexander Communications and Chris Shipley, executive editor of *PC/Computing* Magazine:

- Don't waste the reporter's time. Know what you are going to say and why before you call. Practice with colleagues talking into a phone.
- Don't assume the editor remembers you. Always introduce yourself, your company and your product.
- Don't assume the editor has time to talk. Ask if this is a good time or arrange a time to call back.

Robin Raskin, features editor of *PC Magazine* wants reporters to get to the point quickly. Too much time is wasted on small talk. Although you are merely being polite, avoid asking "Are you busy?"

"I'm always busy. If I say that, they'll be offended. If I don't say it, then they will assume I don't do anything," she said.

If the reporters are not in the office, you can leave a detailed message on the voice mail service. What better way to have your message delivered to the reporters than by your own voice? Tell them everything you would have told them had you reached them. If they are interested, they will call you.

If the reporter doesn't have a voice mail system, you cannot trust the receptionist to leave a detailed message on the "While You Were Out" message pad. There simply isn't enough room. To increase the chances of your message being returned, leave the most important information in as few words as possible. Think of a headline: New product. Appointment for press tour. Arrange demo at convention.

Agency representatives should leave their client's name, not the agency's name. You will make a more dramatic impression by saying Scott Daniels of Widget World, instead of Scott Daniels of ABC Public Relations. The reporter might be interested in Widget World. He or she can only imagine what ABC Public Relations wants to talk about.

Reporters also hate being asked "Did you get my press release?" They get so many press releases, they can't possibly remember any one release. A better strategy is to start with a fresh pitch. That way you can tell your story quickly and clearly. You won't place them in the embarrassing position of saying they don't remember.

Before calling editors, follow these guidelines:

- Don't pitch a product you don't know. Be prepared to answer questions or refer the reporter to the right person. Review the press kit and other material.

- Don't pitch to a magazine you don't know. Read it in advance.

- Don't launch into your pitch and run with it. Give an editor the opportunity to ask questions or direct you to someone else.

- Don't argue with editors. Realize that editors know their publication, its readers and what is appropriate material.

- Don't call on deadline. For weeklies, deadlines are Thursday and Friday. Don't pitch a daily after 2 p.m. Monthly magazines are busiest during the second week of the month. For other details, see Media Map.

- Never, never, never start a conversation with "Did you get my press release." Reporters don't remember the hundreds of releases. If they were interested, they probably would have called you. You should call and provide them with more information or gain their interest.

Let's analyze a 30-second phone pitch. Our purpose is to arrange a meeting with a reviewer. Our phone pitch follows this format and answers these questions.

- Introduction - Who are you and your company?
- Purpose - What are you calling for?
- Positioning Statement - What is your product?
- Interest - How can I help you?
- Answer questions - Do you have any questions?

Introduction

Hello Bill, this is Dan Janal calling about WidgetWorld.

Purpose

Do you have 30 seconds to hear about our newest product?

Reporter: Sure.

Positioning Statement

We are introducing the Widget Utilities. It is a Swiss Army Knife collection of utilities that enhance the performance of widgets.

Interest

You're covering utilities in the December issue, aren't you?

Reporter: Yes. In fact, John Smith should see this too.

Would you like to see a demo? We can be at your office next Monday. Which is better, 10 or 11 a.m.?

Reporter: 10 a.m. looks good.

That's fine. You'll meet with John Cole, the vice president of Widget World. We'll bring our own hardware and give you a copy to review. Do you have any questions?

Answer questions

Reporter: Well, I am interested in the higher level intricacies of arcane formatting techniques. How does your product compare to ZEUS?

I'm not sure about ZEUS. Can I have one of the technicians get back to you on that one?

Reporter: Sure.

Great. We'll see you next Monday at 10 a.m

Now you create your phone pitch.

Phone Pitch Worksheet

1. Introduction - Who are you and your company?

   _____

   _____

   _____

2. Purpose - What are you calling for?

   _____

   _____

   _____

3. Positioning Statement - What is your product?

   _____

   _____

   _____

4. Interest - How can I help you?

   _____

   _____

   _____

5. Answer questions - Do you have any questions?

   _____

   _____

   _____

To help you deal effectively on the phone, read Phone Power by George Walther, Berkley, $3.50, 212-951-8800.

Keep in Touch

Don't let the press forget who you are. Call them periodically. However, don't try to become their best friend overnight. That takes time. Develop rapport first. If things click, then feel free to call any time. If you don't get a good feel, call only when you have news.

In addition, don't call aimlessly. Have a goal in mind. Call to find out what stories they are writing about in the next few months or what progress they are making reviewing your product. You can discuss:

- What's new in the industry.
- What your company is doing.
- What is new in your market segment.

Because your time is limited as is their patience, you should prioritize your calls. Create a chart that reminds you who to call and when to call them. This way you can stay in touch with everyone who is important.

Now its your turn. (You get the idea now!) Remember to prioritize. Weekly calls correspond to the A List. Monthly calls go to the B List. Quarterly calls go to the C List.

Phone Contact Worksheet

Weekly (A list)	Publication	Reporter	Telephone
_____			
_____			
_____			
_____			
_____			
_____			
_____			

Monthly (B list)

_____
_____
_____
_____
_____
_____

Quarterly (C list)

_____
_____
_____
_____
_____

Help Reporters Write the Story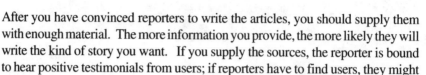

After you have convinced reporters to write the articles, you should supply them with enough material. The more information you provide, the more likely they will write the kind of story you want. If you supply the sources, the reporter is bound to hear positive testimonials from users; if reporters have to find users, they might find people who are not 100 percent pleased. By controlling the flow of information, you can help create a positive, upbeat story that will help sales.

Reporters need:

- Technical facts
- Testimonials by users
- Marketing details

Some reporters need more information because they write for highly technical magazines or because they want to gather fresh quotes and new material so their story doesn't look like the one written by another magazine to whom you pitched the article. Be prepared by knowing all you can about these topics. Just in case, create a list of people and phone numbers who can answer the difficult questions.

For instance, *PC Week* routinely asks for the names and phone numbers of three users whenever they write a product focus.

Editorial Follow-up Worksheet

	Person	Phone number
Product Manager		
Marketing Manager		
Technical Manager		
User 1		
User 2		
User 3		
Analyst 1		
Analyst 2		

By creating this simple chart, you will feel comfortable when you deal with the toughest reporter.

Get Messages Answered: Use MCI Mail

Analyst Stewart Alsop is on the road more often than he is in his office. He checks for his messages and returns the most important ones. However, he can be reached anytime, anywhere, anyplace by sending messages via MCI Mail. MCI Mail is an electronic message service you can use with a computer, modem, communications software and an account with MCI Mail service.

He always responds quickly, if not always favorably.

One of the best ways to reach reporters is by sending messages through MCI Mail. This must be one of the best-kept secrets in PR because so few practitioners use MCI Mail.

Using this electronic mailbox service is the surest way of getting the reporters' attentions because:

- It bypasses the stack of pink "While You Were Out" message slips.
- It bypasses the stack of incoming press releases.
- You can send a receipt with the message that tells you when the reporter read the memo.
- You can reach reporters when they are on the road.
- Most reporters like getting MCI Mail and respond quickly and politely, if not always affirmatively. Scott Mace of *InfoWorld* takes the matter a step further. He invites electronic press releases and looks forward to the time when paper press releases won't exist.

Invariably, you will get a quick response from the editor because answering is simple and electronic communication is brief, with short sentences and a lack of formality, which increases the likelihood of a response. By using MCI Mail, you show you actually use the technology, which builds your credibility.

There is an etiquette about using MCI. Use short (100 word) messages. Never, never, never send an unsolicited press release. Use a 100-word pitch letter only. Don't badger reporters. (For example: When are you going to review my product?) MCI Mail is great for sending quick pitch letters, follow up letters and thank-you notes. Don't use MCI Mail for longer documents such as press releases, press kits and backgrounders unless the reporter asks for it. Avoid writing long letters (anything longer than 24 lines is long. That is the amount of space it takes to fill one computer screen. Any note longer than a screen is considered too long).

You'll also save time on postage, mailing and filing — and you usually get through to your reporters. What could be easier?

Everyone who uses MCI Mail has an address box, which corresponds to the person's name. That makes it easy to find editors. If you wanted to send me a letter, you would merely address it to Daniel Janal. In some cases, a person's name is truncated to the first initial of the first name and the full last name, i.e., DJANAL. In rarer cases, the name of the magazine is the only way to reach the reporter: Electronic Business. Sometimes you might type the name of a reporter and MCI will tell you that there is more than one person with that name. This means the reporter has a private account and a company account:

TIP

Use MCI Mail to bypass a mountain of pink "While you were out" message slips.

Robin Raskin, New York, NY, or

Robin Raskin, PC Magazine, New York, NY.

When you have the choice, send mail to the magazine address. When reporters respond, they will do so at the magazine's expense, a great savings for them.

For a full explanation on how to use MCI Mail, read *The Complete MCI Mail Handbook* by Stephen Manes, Bantam Computer Books, $22.95. It includes a $10 discount off MCI's $25 annual fee.

MCI Mail costs $25 per year to subscribe. There is no charge for receiving mail or checking your mailbox.

The price for sending messages is based on characters in the note (6 characters equals 1 word, on the average):

up to 500 characters	45 cents
501 to 2500 characters	75 cents
2501-7500 characters	1.00
each additional 7500 characters	1.00

You can also send facsimiles via MCI Mail if your text is in ASCII format. The procedure is very easy. The prices are:

first half page	50 cents
additional half pages	30 cents

To order, call 1-800-444-6245. In Washington, D.C., call 833-8484.

Get the Fax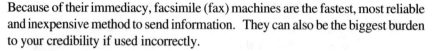

Because of their immediacy, facsimile (fax) machines are the fastest, most reliable and inexpensive method to send information. They can also be the biggest burden to your credibility if used incorrectly.

The best policy is to call the reporter, gain interest and then ask if you can send a fax. Always double check the fax number against any printed reference number because some receivers, flooded with unsolicited faxes, change their numbers every week or month.

Follow these tips:

- Never send a fax unless the reporter requests it.
- Never send faxes longer than five pages (excluding cover sheet).
- Never send faxes with lists of other reporters receiving it
- Write any notes on the cover page to save transmission time and paper.

Because fax machines print at a barely readable 200 dots per inch, take these precautions to ensure the document is as legible as possible:

- Print in boldface.
- Use larger sized type (12 point).
- Double space between lines.
- Indicate how many pages will be sent.
- List name and phone number of person to call in case of trouble.
- Call to confirm only if you think there might be a problem.

By following these tips, your faxes — and your messages — will be well received.

Software Review Policies

Once you send software or a book to a reviewer, kiss it goodbye. Reporters don't return software.

Some companies send software to every reporter on their A list, whether requested or not. The advantage of this strategy is that reporters get the software without the trouble of picking up the phone to order it. The disadvantages are the extra costs of product and shipping, as well as not knowing if the software will be reviewed.

While we don't recommend sending software out to hundreds of reporters at a time, there is a benefit to sending unrequested copies to the top reviewers.

We sent a copy of AXE, a file compression program published by System Enhancement Associates, to John Dvorak, a key reviewer and columnist. He raved about the software and called it "truly exceptional." Sales soared. A publisher called to buy limited rights to resell it under a different name. A product was born.

PC Hardware Review Policies

Before sending out PC computer hardware, you should have a review policy in place to secure its return. Otherwise, you might lose thousands of dollars of products. A sample hardware review request form follows. After the reporter returns the signed form, you can freely send the material.

We generally recommend loaning a product like an add-on board or an internal product for 30 or 90 days.

If the reporter has not sent the hardware back, don't worry. He probably isn't trying to steal it. Chances are he hasn't finished his review and needs to keep the product a few weeks longer. Call a week before the due date to see if he has any questions, needs the product longer, or requires shipping instructions.

Sometimes, a reporter will fall in love with your product and not want to return it. Many manufacturers have press prices for their products. The price is generally the same as the dealer price or just a little bit more so the company can't be accused of undercutting their dealers.

Just as with any follow up, you should call reporters to see if they have received the hardware, have any questions, need photos and when the review should appear.

Request for Hardware for Editorial Review

I agree to review the products identified on this form and return them within 90 days to the address listed on this form.   COMPANY will pay shipping costs.

If I fail to return the products within that time frame, my company will be sent an invoice for the dealer cost of the products.

I understand I am not obligated to write about these products in any way.

The products are:

Model_____   Serial number:_____

Model_____   Serial number:_____

Model_____   Serial number:_____

Model_____   Serial number:_____

_____

Editor

_____

Publication

_____

Address

_____

City, State   Zip

_____

Phone

Return products to:

YOUR COMPANY

Attn: Product loan department

Address

City, State, Zip

How to Follow Up with Reviewers

About two weeks after you have sent out the hardware or software, call reviewers and see what they're doing. You want to accomplish these tasks:

- Make sure they received the product.
- Ensure it works.
- See how and when they plan to review it.
- Find out if they have any problems.
- Provide general troubleshooting.

When a publicist followed up, the reviewer said: "I put it in and it didn't work right, so I'm not using your product any more."

The publicist had to motivate him to do that and suggest that he review the product in its own environment.

The publicist gathered the information about the problem, said he would check with the technical staff and reminded the reporter of his initial interest in the product and its benefits. He found the answers to the questions, called the reviewer and give him the information. A positive review followed.

If the problem is too technical for you to discuss, have the support department call the reporter and answer his questions. Follow up with the support person to make sure he actually called. Then call the reporter to see if he has other questions. You can't afford to lose the review after you've gone this far. These steps can mean the difference between success and failure.

By staying in touch with the reviewer and find out if problems exist, you will increase chances of getting a review.

Responding to Errors

The review appears. That's the good news. There's an inaccuracy. That's the bad news. What do you do?

If there is a factual problem, write a letter to the editor and provide the correct information. Magazine are willing to correct their mistakes. To help prevent those mistakes, try to double check facts with reporters. Double check prices and phone numbers.

Some magazines, like *Home Office Computing* and *PC Week*, have editors who check every word that will appear. They will call you to check every fact in the article. However, they won't let you see the article or comment on reporters' opinions.

Few magazines will send a copy of the article to you before it has been printed. That's because they don't want the manufacturer to dispute every word.

Magazines work under tight deadlines and don't spend the time to fact check every article with the sources. Most magazines do not employ fact checkers. That is a sad fact, but true. That means errors will appear in print. Be ready to take positive steps to correct errors while still maintaining positive relations with reporters.

Responding to Good Reviews

If the review is good, how do you show your appreciation to the reporter? Is it a good idea to send a thank you note, a gift, or make dinner reservations to indicate your appreciation?

Never, ever, ever send a gift. Magazines have policies prohibiting their reporters from receiving gifts. Some people, however, do send flowers to reporters.

You can arrange a lunch meeting. This is a nice gesture and solves two functions: Reporters can do their jobs keeping in contact with sources. The meal does not violate the strict ethical code many magazines have created for their editors that prohibit them from accepting gifts. You can keep them up to date on developments.

In any case, a thank-you note is always appropriate.

Responding to Bad Reviews

What happens when a review finds fault?

Maybe they are right.

Perhaps your idea is only half baked. Or overworked. Or the product really has an unusable interface. It is not the end of the world. You must have the ability to look objectively at the review and cull out the things that the reviewer sees as being truly positive. Positive because you can work to enhance those features.

Maybe that's why reporters wondered if there was a market. Perhaps the reviewer has a point. Think about it. In any case, don't buy a gun. And don't fire your PR person. Don't kill the messenger.

If you disagree with their opinion, bite your tongue. You can't argue an opinion. You should never argue with people who buy ink by the barrel.

Instead, do your best to mend fences. Call or write the reviewers and tell them you appreciate their comments and that the company is striving to address those issues in making the product. That way, they will be more receptive to reviewing the revised edition.

Some people think magazines write only generally positive reviews. That is not necessarily true. Some will call 'em as they see 'em. However, some will only write about product they truly recommend. If editors tell you they won't write about your product, don't push them. They might be doing you a favor by not printing a damaging negative review.

Finally, reviewers just might be wrong and there is nothing you can do. Recently, a product was panned in *PC Magazine*. The editor liked the product, a computerized shorthand program, but thought there was no need for this product category. The review did say the program was useful in some applications, so the company could capitalize on that. He also misunderstood the market in which the product was successful.

The company wrote a letter pointing out this information in a friendly manner and invited him to see a demo of the future version. The editor was willing.

By being polite and factual, the company built a positive relationship and perhaps, get a better review in the future.

The very next day, *Personal Computing* and *Home Office Computing* rated that product as one of the best of the year.

There's no accounting for taste.

Ensuring Everyone Sees the Review

The real value in a review, product announcement or news story is not merely in who reads the story in that sitting. It is in the ability to send that article the next day, the next week, the next month and the next year to anyone you choose - your dealers, salespeople, new leads, contacts, venture capital people and industry colleagues.

Reprint every good piece. It helps to build momentum. You can include the reprint with a cover letter, with your ad or with other company literature that you send to dealers, distributors, analysts, opinion leaders, new business prospects, current clients and reporters. When you do, you improve the credibility of the company and its products.

Reprint Rights

To stay on the right side of the law, you should call the magazine to get the right to reprint the article. Some magazines also will reprint the article for you (quite expensively, but quite nicely). You can buy the reprint right and have your local printer print thousands of copies.

To obtain permission, write a letter stating the issue, page number, article name and purpose for the reprint. Here are a few policies from the top computer publications.

PC Magazine – Rights cost $40. Call Paula Botts — 212-503-5448. Printing prices vary, call Jennifer Locke — 212-503-5447. Reprints are custom-designed. Price depends on the article and amount of work to create the reprint. 500 copies minimum.

BYTE – Prices for rights vary by article and use and can be as high as $100 per page of text. Contact Faith Cluntz — 603-924-2525. Printing depends on size and quantity. 500 copies minimum.

Home Office Computing – Rights cost $80 per page. Contact Mike Espindo — 212-505-3577. Printing prices vary. Contact David Lang — 212-505-3579. HOC can print them in-house (no minimum number of copies) or deliver negatives of the pages to you to print.

MACWORLD – Rights cost $50. Contact Joyce Ripp — 415-978-3235. Printing cost for a standard 8-page feature, 500 copies would be $263 for black and white, $908 in color and must be placed through MacWorld.

InfoWorld – *InfoWorld* does not give permission to reprint articles. However, it will print black and white or color articles for a fee and will print your logo for free. Contact Stephanie Beach — 1-800-227-8365.

Below is a sample letter requesting rights.

May 26, 1990

Lisa Fountis
Marketing Services Department
CMP Publications
600 Community Drive
Manhasset, NY 11030

Dear Ms. Fountis:

We would like permission to reprint an article that appeared in Electronic Engineering Times on January 12, 1990 on page 33. The article was entitled "Handy Scanner is a Bargain."

We have enclosed a copy of the article.

We will use the reprint for promotional purposes.

Enclosed is a check for $35 for the rights to reprint the article.

Thank you,

Daniel Janal
President

ENCLOSURES
DSJ/rrr

Hit the Road

Visiting publications' offices to demonstrate the product to reporters or editors enhances the chances of getting a product reviewed. You can operate under ideal conditions: their turf, your equipment, your expertise, no time pressure.

Reporters usually are happy to watch a new product for a half hour. If you are lucky, several reporters might sit in. When ECA Computer and Communications Products arranged to demonstrate the A4 Color Hand Scanner to a news reporter from *InfoWorld,* the review editor and two other reporters dropped in. These contacts produced a news article in the next week's issue. The same thing happened when they visited *Publish* and *PC World.*

To set up a road show, determine which magazines would benefit you the most. Road shows can be expensive, with airfare, hotel rooms and staff time, so you want to allocate your resources wisely.

Here is a sample checklist of media that cover most general interest computer products. To control costs, conduct road shows to targeted areas of the country that have the most press in a centralized location. These areas generally are New York, Boston/New Hampshire, San Francisco and Washington, D.C.

Place a priority number next to the magazines that reach your audience, or fill in the blanks with other magazines or analysts for this sample agenda for a business software product or hardware product:

New York

❑ PC Magazine

❑ Computer Shopper

❑ Computer Buyers Guide & Handbook

❑ Computers in Accounting

❑ Computer Reseller News

❑ VAR Business

❑ Electronic Engineering Times

❑ Home Office Computing

❑ PC Sources

Boston/New Hampshire

- ❑ PC Week
- ❑ PC Computing
- ❑ Lotus Magazine
- ❑ BIS CAP (analysts)
- ❑ Byte
- ❑ PC Laptop
- ❑ Macworld
- ❑ Soft·Letter (analyst)
- ❑ IDC (analysts)

San Francisco

- ❑ PC World
- ❑ InfoWorld
- ❑ Publish
- ❑ Macworld
- ❑ Dr. John Heilborn Syndicated Columnist
- ❑ PC Letter (analyst) Stewart Alsop
- ❑ Creative Strategies (analyst) Tim Bajarin

Washington, D.C.

- ❑ Government Computer News
- ❑ Federal Computer Week
- ❑ InfoWorld (Baltimore)

Call reporters about a month before you want to demonstrate the product. Don't call on deadline day. Check to see whether a major convention is scheduled during your tour, as it will steal away reporters and editors who might want to see your product. (See the phone pitching workshop to prepare your discussion.) Send a confirmation note and press materials immediately to your interviewer. The confirmation note should have the name of the company representatives, their titles, the scope of interview or demo, the time, date and place for the appointment and other information that sparks their interest.

July 24, 1990

Mr. Preston Gralla
PC Computing
4 Cambridge Center,
9th Floor
Cambridge, MA 02142

Dear Mr. Gralla:

This note will confirm your appointment with ECA Computer and Communications Products on Wednesday, August 13 at 11 a.m. in your offices.

You will meet with Frank Tzeng, associate president, who will demonstrate the new BONA Lan Fax Server. We will gear the demo toward your interest in network management issues. You'll find the press release and price sheets for the products in this package.

Please call me if you have any questions.

Sincerely yours,

Daniel Janal
President

ENCLOSURE

DSJ/rrr

Get directions, including estimates of how long it will take to drive from one office to the next. Always schedule extra time between appointments; for some reason, demos always take longer than planned, especially if the press is really interested in the product. Plan on spending 30 minutes demonstrating the product. Now add another 10 minutes to set up the computer and put the parts back in boxes.

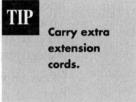

TIP

Carry extra extension cords.

Bring your own equipment, including a monitor to get the best visual display. If you bring your own equipment, everything will run smoothly. There is nothing more disturbing than finding your add-in board upsets the dip switch settings of magazine's computers. Some magazines won't even let you place hardware or software in their computers. Others have monitors that look like dirt. These machines will negatively affect the reporters' perceptions of your products.

Take several extra copies of your press kits, photos of screens and products in case extra reporters attend the meeting.

Carry final copies of the product. Bring the same materials a consumer would find when buying the product. Some magazines will work with beta copies, but many want to see the final product.

The best preparation for a successful road show begins at home. Conduct a sample demo in front of fellow workers at your company. Let them critique your presentation.

Reporters follow one of these personalities:

- Student.
- Inquisitive.
- Prosecutor.
- Consultant.

Students sit still during the entire presentation. They rarely ask questions. When the demo is over, they ask a few questions. They are generally not well informed about the product category. They sit, learn and ask basic questions.

Inquisitive reporters generally let you follow your script, but ask intelligent questions.

Prosecutors have their own game plan in mind before you get there. They know the product category and constantly ask questions.

Consultants think they know more about the product and marketing than you do. They continually comment about each feature and tell you how it can be improved, co-marketed, bundled or forgotten.

Be prepared by practicing for each type of interview. Don't get flustered by naive questions or by someone telling you how to run your business. Be flexible so you can adapt your presentation to fit the needs of each reporter.

After finishing the demo, follow a step from the salesperson: ask for the order. Ask reporters if they plan to review the product, whether it will be stand-alone or group roundup, when the article will appear, what additional material is needed, such as photographs, names and phone numbers of users.

Follow up with a thank-you note and provide the extra material the reporter requested.

When to Give Exclusives

Some magazines want exclusive editorial rights to your company's new products so they can claim to be the most important and current periodical. They will repay you with special coverage and treatment, which might include a cover story and photographs of your product. This high level of exposure can help promote your product greatly.

To arrange exclusive, call your contact at a monthly magazine at least six months in advance of the announced shipping date of your product. This will give the editor time to coordinate editorial coverage. If you are granting the exclusive to a weekly publication, call them about six weeks ahead of the ship date.

These magazines will be willing to sign non-disclosure forms that prohibit them from revealing the information before the agreed-upon date. A sample non-disclosure form appears at the end of this chapter.

Some publications do not grant exclusives. When they find news, they print it. They live in mortal fear that another publication will find out about the news and print it before they can. Ask the editor if he will respect your wishes before you disclose the information. Also, don't ever say something and then tell the editor the comment is off the record. The game isn't played that way. You should rarely use say something off the record because some reporters do not honor off the record, or they forget what was said on the record and off the record. Some spokespersons and reporters play games within the boundaries of acceptable behavior when they allow comments to be attributed to "a company spokesperson" or "a source close to the company." Use these ploys when you want to get your message across, but want to shield the person who said it. Politicians do this all the time (A source close to the investigation, a source close to the White House.") It has little place in high tech publicity. Information should be open and honest or not told at all.

Sample Non-disclosure Form

DATE

I agree to not tell anyone about ......product or code name.......produced by ....company..........until the product is officially announced by the company.

This constitutes the entire agreement.   For the vendor, supplier, agent, consultant:

_____

Signed

_____

Printed

_____

Title

_____

Company

_____

Date

For the company:

_____

Signed

_____

Printed

_____

Title

_____

Company

_____

Date

Great Expectations

You should begin seeing articles in print as soon as a week after the demonstration in weekly newspapers and daily newspaper columns. Monthly magazines can take from three to four months before printing news articles.

Reviews can take much longer. In one case, Bill Machrone saw a demo of PRD+, a computerized shorthand program, in May and reviewed it in December.

There is no way to speed up the review process. If you go over reporters' heads, you will lose them as contacts. If you threaten to withhold advertising, you will brand yourself as an amateur. Remain calm, call reporters every few weeks to keep them up to date on upgrades.

Monitoring Results

No matter how hard you scour publications, you are bound to miss articles mentioning your company and its products.

Not to worry. You can hire a "clipping service" to clip articles about your company and its products. Clipping bureaus read and clip all important business, trade, consumer magazines and the top daily newspapers. They can also monitor television, radio and international publications. The three largest clipping services are Bacon's, Burrelle's and Luce. They charge roughly the same amount and provide about the same quality of service.

You will pay a reading charge of $180-200 a month and a about $1 for each article they clip. They don't call them clipping services for nothing. However, the cost of the service is offset by the cost of the magazines you would have to purchase as well as the time and effort to read and clip each article.

The clipping services generally send articles to you once a week. Each article is cut from the magazine and identified with a note sized piece of paper listing the magazine, publication date and circulation.

Sources:

Bacon's Clipping Service,
332 S. Michigan Avenue, Chicago, IL 60604, (312) 922-2400.

Burrelle's,
75 E. Northfield Road, Livingston, NJ 07039, (201) 992-6600 or 1-800-631-1160

Luce Press Clippings,
Lexington Avenue, New York, NY 10170, (212) 889-6711 or 1-800-528-8226

Several electronic services can help you find clips and find information on competitors. The Ziff Davis Computer Library lists full text articles from 130 high tech magazines. You can find information by typing in the name of the company, product or magazine. It is available by calling CompuServe, an online data network. To subscribe to CompuServe, call 1-800-848-8199. The rates are $6.50 per hour. Once you have a subscription, you will be able to use the Computer Library, which carries these basic charges: 40 cents per minute to use the service plus: $2.50 for complete record or $1 for abstract only.

Even clipping services can't guarantee 100 percent service. They can — and even claim to —miss as many as 20 percent of the articles. However, they can provide a level of service that is better than you can provide yourself.

SECTION 2

Conventional Wisdom: How to Publicize Products and Services at Conventions

Conventions are the most cost-effective method to publicize high tech products. Here are strategies and action plans to ensure that you achieve maximum coverage.

Publicize Products at Conventions

Conventions and trade shows offer the greatest opportunity to get press coverage for technology companies. Imagine 400-500 of the most influential reporters from the key magazines being in the same city and hotel for a week — and their assignment is to find out what is new and interesting. Remember, they need you as much as you need them! They have to fill thousands of pages with news and are eager to find interesting stories. Your job is to make the story interesting.

This section will share techniques and strategies for getting noticed at some of the largest trade shows in the world. It is easy for people and products to get lost but you'll be armed with successful strategies after reading this section.

The payoff is great. News articles in trade publications can lead to thousands of requests for product information and thousands of orders. Products can become an overnight sensation if you follow the right strategy. Or they can die an obscure death if you don't.

There are many opportunities to talk to the press at a convention. You can demonstrate your product to reporters while they are receptive. You can talk as reporters walk about the convention floor or stand in line for the taxi ride to a party. No other gathering offers as many opportunities for press contact as a convention.

The strategies you will learn will work at the largest computer trade show, Comdex, with 100,000 attendees and 1,000 reporters, as well as at regional and local trade shows and computer fairs.

PR Overview

An effective publicity campaign begins at home. Ninety percent of your work is done before you ever set foot on the airplane that takes you to Chicago, Las Vegas, Atlanta, New York or wherever your trade show is.

You must:

- Determine your message.
- Create press kits to deliver your message.
- Select the media you should tell you message to.
- Decide which vehicle should be used to disseminate the message (press conference, interviews, hospitality suites, etc.).
- Determine the action you want the reporters to take (for example, news articles, product reviews, industry analysis articles, and/orbuilding relationships with the press).

Many of these tasks can be performed by using the workshop sheets in the first section. Make copies of those blank worksheets whenever you need to plan your trade show activities so you can plan for many events.

Determine Which Shows to Attend

Just as you must match your message to appropriate editors, so must you pick trade shows that reach your desired audience. Before going to a show, check the show's demographics so you can be assured of picking the show that will reach your target market.

How do you find information?

Every trade show has a sales office that clearly tracks the demographics of the audience. This information will include:

- Number of attendees.
- Job titles.
- Buying power.

If you study these numbers, you will find the greatest opportunities to invest your money and time. You'll be able to see whether the show fits the profile of the audiences you want to reach. The report also will say how many reporters attended the last show. You can also call key reporters and ask them which shows they attend.

Check the show's track record. Talk to previous exhibitors and listen to their stories. Call your target reporters and ask them if they will attend.

Find out what the show will do to promote and attract attendees. This is especially important at regional meetings and new shows.

Media Map publishes the Trade Show Report, $795, which compiles demographics for 50 computer related trade shows. It includes an overview of each show, the show dates, management, sponsor, analysis of attendees and exhibitors, press opportunities and other logistics and services. For another 150 shows, it lists show dates, audience, attendance figures and an overview. (Media Map, 130 The Great Road, Bedford, MA 01730, 617-275-5560.)

By doing your homework, you'll discover which shows fit your needs.

Other Agendas for Trade Shows

While you are at a trade show, you can perform many activities to build your business. Used properly, a trade show not only increases your press coverage, but also creates the opportunity to foster relationships with key players in the industry such as analysts, distributors and other opinion leaders.

Conventions are great places to meet people. People go to trade shows to be seen. If you're not at a trade show, people wonder, "Gee, what happened to Joe? He must not be around any more."

By going to trade shows and going to the right parties at trade shows, people see you are in circulation. You will promote your credibility. One public relations goals is to keep your name in front of people. That way, whenever they need your services, they will think of you.

Another reason to attend trade shows is to see what your competitors are doing. You can walk into the booth, get a demo, ask tough questions and get meaningful answers. All this information is public, so don't feel you are doing anything underhanded. They won't tell you anything they aren't telling their key accounts and dealers. And you will benefit from knowing their latest plans. You can see how they are positioning themselves and the kinds of materials they give out.

You'll benefit if you copy the activities and materials you like and avoid the things that don't work. By keeping notes, you'll have a file to refer to when you are ready to exhibit, or revise your exhibit for the next convention.

Get Free Info from the Press Office

The conference's press office can provide a wealth of free information. A good sponsor will provide many services for your public relations efforts. Among those services are:

- Press lists–complete registration list of attending media, with office phone numbers. Use this list to quickly determine who should see your product.

- Press conference schedule–listing all the available times for press conferences. Use this list to determine the best time for your press confer ence. You don't want to compete with IBM's press conference because no one will attend yours.

- Show catalogue–contains a short description of the products your com pany will exhibit.

- Show newspaper–prints articles and pictures of products introduced at the show.

These services are free to exhibitors. onl.y. If you are not exhibiting, your job will be harder. Harder, but not impossible. That's because you have created media lists, determined your positioning statement and know which press covers your market.

If you work with the show office, you'll get lots of useful information and extra coverage.

How to Increase Pre-show Coverage

Your company can get press coverage even before the show begins. This strategy will help you create booth traffic among attendees and generate excitement from other reporters who will be more inclined to visit your booth because you have been blessed with editorial credibility.

Many shows publish newspapers that are given free to conventioneers. For example, The Interface Group, which runs Comdex, sends a newspaper containing articles about new products that will be introduced at the show to potential registrants about two months before the show.

To be included in the show daily newspapers, follow these steps. When you register for the show, find out who edits the show daily. Comdex maintains its own editorial offices, while PC Expo farms out the newspaper. Call the editor and find out the deadlines. PC Expo is about six weeks before the show. Comdex is at the show itself. Supply the editor with the material well in advance of the deadlines to give them enough time.

As with press releases, you want to tell the reporter what is new about your product. Keep in mind the differences between features and benefits.

TIP

A photo increases the chances of getting coverage in a show daily. Send one to the editor.

A photo increases the chances of getting coverage in a show daily. Send one to the editor.

Several publications print special show issues that describe interesting products that will be introduced at the show. Call *InfoWorld*, *PC Week*, *Computer Reseller News* and other publications to ensure your product is previewed.

By following these strategies, you will help to build booth traffic at the show.

Luring Reporters to See Your Product ■

Calling editors for appointments is truly a new art form.

You have four goals:

- Confirm appointments for the reporter to see a demo of the product or interview executives.

- If reporters are busy, try to get them to agree to stop by the booth at their convenience.

- Ask the reporter to write an article for the show edition of the paper.

- Ask the reporter to set up an appointment to see the product in the office before or after the show.

Getting a confirmed appointment at a convention can be difficult because the press has to see a great many things.

Put yourself in the mind of reporters. They have to cover the entire show and the press conferences. They aren't sure when the press conferences are being held, because the show office won't release the final schedule until the show starts. They have a few appointments already scheduled with the biggest companies in the industry. They aren't sure where they will be in relation to your booth simply because of logistics.

Some reporters might politely say "Well, I don't have my press conference list, and I want to see what else is going on at the show, but I'll try to stop by."

This is not a put off. Reporters want to see as much of the show as they can and will walk up and down every aisle. When they see your booth, it will click, and they will say, "Aha, this product sticks in my mind, I want to see what this thing is."

Don't despair, you can get appointments. Follow this battle plan.

Your first attempt should always be to try to get confirmed appointments with the press to attend demos of your product. By setting confirmed interviews, you can be reasonable assured that the press will attend your demo, party or press conference. If they see the demonstration and are impressed, they probably will write about the product.

Setting confirmed interviews also helps you schedule executives and technicians who need to be on hand for the demo.

Begin calling reporters about one month before the event.

Even if reporters just say they will stop by the booth, you've won on two levels. You've educated them. That's a very important process. Even if you can't pin them down to a time, they know about your company. They know about your product. Second, if you can't meet them at the show, you can set a time to meet them in their offices after the show to demo the product. If your product is hot, you might want to visit the editor BEFORE the show and demonstrate the product. Demonstrating the product at the editors' offices is prefered because the meeting will be free of interruptions and distractions from a convention.

A word about appointments. Many confirmed appointments will be late or reporters won't show up. This is not a slap in the face. Reporters honestly get sidetracked when they see something glitzy. They can also run behind their schedules either because appointments are running late or they can't hail a taxi to your site. Don't be disturbed.

Warn your executives and demo personnel that the reporter might be late. They shouldn't get uptight, because that tenseness will come through in an interview or demo.

With all the commotion at a convention, it is easy for appointments to get lost in the shuffle. Don't let that appointment be yours. Here's a two-step program that reduces no-shows to a minimum developed by PR professional Joel Strasser, the "dean" of high tech publicists.

1. When you schedule the appointment, ask the reporter for the hotel he or she will staying in and the phone number.

2. The night before the appointment, call the hotel and leave a message with the hotel message center. Don't call the reporter's room. You might wake him or her! When the reporter checks messages that night or in the morning, he or she will be reminded of the appointment.

Now that you have the appointment, where do you meet the reporter?

You have four choices:

1. At the booth. This is a good place to demo the product as you have all your equipment and experts in one place. If you have a big booth, design a meeting room so you can have privacy and quiet when you talk to the reporter. If the booth doesn't have a meeting room, the demo could get crowded with other observers. Designate one computer as the VIP area and alert booth personnel to leave you alone. You don't want the reporter to feel pressed for time or space.

You must be on your best behavior. Don't come on too strong. Reporters will be intimidated and will turn you off. Act as a consultant and advisor.

2. At the press room. Most conventions have a room set aside for the press to conduct interviews. You must bring your own equipment to demonstrate your product, however, as most press rooms lack fully configured computers. Check with the show office before selecting the press room. If your company does not have a booth, this is the preferred strategy.

3. At your hospitality suite. If you don't want to pay for booth space, consider renting a hotel room in a nearby hotel and setting up a hospitality suite. This strategy gives you the luxury of controlling the environment for the demo, from lighting to beverages. You also will be assured the computer works and that the reporter won't be distracted, which could happen in a booth. However, if your hospitality suite is not within walking distance of the convention center, the press might be reluctant to visit because it takes a long time to find a taxi, travel to your room, and return to the convention. Only the biggest companies with the hottest products can attract many reporters this way. However, you might consider piggybacking with other companies that use hospitality suites. For instance, if you know a big company is having a hospitality suite in the Waldorf Astoria, the press will come to it. You might rent a suite in that hotel and tell the media they can see your product before or after they see the bigger company. Rick Doherty of *Electronic Engineering Times* said he combines trips. He sees the show the first day and then spends the rest of the time visiting hospitality suites.

> **TIP**
> Mealtimes are great times to set appointments. Breakfast and supper meetings are good times to talk to key editors as they provide a quiet time before or after the show to relax and concentrate on your story.

4. At a restaurant. As with the hospitality suite, only the biggest companies can lure a reporter away for lunch. Breakfast and dinner are the best times. The pluses are that you will have the reporter's attention. If your purpose is to establish good rapport and conduct an interview about marketing or finance, then a restaurant meeting is clearly appropriate. If your product runs on a laptop, you'll be able to do a competent demo. The minuses are that you have to bring you equipment to the restaurant, which undoubtedly won't have suitable accommodations for a full demo. If you must depend on a crisp monitor, input devices and printers, you won't be able to do a solid demo. Meals, however, are fine for interviews or to establish rapport with reporters.

Some people say that the quickest way to reporters' editorial pages is through their stomachs. That's not necessarily true. There is so much free food at a trade show that another round of hors d'oeuvres does not necessarily motivate a reporter to talk to you.

However, there is no denying that mealtimes are great times to set appointments. Breakfast and supper meetings are good times to talk to key editors as they provide a quiet time before or after the show to relax and concentrate on your story. Lunches should be avoided as they take too much time from the middle of the day.

Avoid eating messy food. Even Ricardo Montalban would look like Danny de Vito when eating French onion soup.

By the way, you pick up the tab, not the reporter. IBM made this fatal mistake when they dined with columnist John Dvorak. He had the last word. Dvorak blasted IBM in a full-page column in *PC Magazine.*

How to Get Press Coverage
If You Don't Rent a Booth

Renting a booth can be very expensive and well beyond the means of many start-up companies. Trade shows still can be a fruitful public relations medium, however, even if you are without portfolio (so to speak).

The first thing you must realize is the press doesn't care if you have a booth. It is not a sign of wealth or poverty. However, it might be a sign of good marketing.

For instance, Peter Norton Computing doesn't exhibit at Comdex. But it does host a hospitality suite and a breakfast for user groups.

Guerilla marketing strategies without a booth include meetings in hospitality suites, pre-arranged meetings in the press room, talking to press outside other companies' press conferences and other strategies that will be discussed in greater detail in the next chapters.

In fact, armed with a laptop computer and a chair, you can demo a program to reporters while standing outside the press room or in a hallway.

This is exactly how Ken Skier's No-Squint Laptop Cursor conducted a 10-second demo to dozens of reporters at a recent Comdex. Reporters grasped the concept immediately. Seeing is believing. Reporters received the software and walked away with enough information to write an article or review. Reporters from many leading magazines wrote about the product.

Set a Realistic Budget

How much money should you spend on publicity for a trade show? It depends on how much you can afford and how much you should afford. You don't have to have an enormous budget in order to make an impact, particularly if you're just getting started.

It is more important to be smart and aggressive than to have a lot of money. You have to know what the press wants. If you make their jobs easier by providing good stories with appropriate background, you'll get your rewards.

There are two ways to set budgets. Standard rules of thumb hold that a public relations budget should be 1 percent of sales. This percentage can differ depending on your product, its niche, or issues of timing.

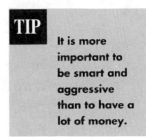

TIP

It is more important to be smart and aggressive than to have a lot of money.

Another way to set budgets is with a flat rate. Soft•Letter conducted a study in 1989 that showed small to medium sized software publishing companies spent between $2,000 and $3,000 a month. Larger companies spent considerably more. (Soft•Letter, 17 Main Street, Watertown, MA 02172, 617-924-3944.)

To put matters in perspective, think about how much ads cost in your target magazines(usually $5,000-25,000). Now figure how much a review would be worth to you in those magazines. So when you talk to public relations agencies or plan your budget, put everything into perspective.

Budget Worksheet

Here is a listing of typical expense items:

Professional fees (for agency personnel)	_____
Senior level	_____
Junior level	_____
Phone	_____
MCI Mail	_____
CompuServe	_____
Fax	_____
Postage	_____
Courier Services (Federal Express)	_____
Printing	_____
Stationery	_____
Envelopes	_____
Press kit covers	_____
Stickers	_____
Posters	_____
Travel and Entertainment	_____
Meals with reporters	_____
Travel to and from airports	_____
Taxis	_____
Incidentals	_____
Total	_____

Convention Action plan

This section will focus executing these strategies and will offer other guerilla strategies to improve press coverage of your company's products. Here is an outline of suggested activities you should perform to improve your chances of getting noticed.

- **Logistics**

    Place press kits in press kit room.

    Post press release on bulletin board in press room.

    Keep a supply of press kits in the booth.

    Hold a handful of press kits with you.

    Collect business cards/write follow-up notes on them.

    Post notices of press conferences, hospitality suites or booths in or near the press room.

    Find the rooms where reporters congregate (press room, press conference rooms).

    Confirm appointments.

- **Media**

    Confirmed interviews

    Call reporter's hotel the night before to confirm.

    Come to meeting site 10 minutes before appointment.

    Wait 15 minutes past appointed time for late editors.

On-the-spot interviews

Stand outside press room with press kits.

Read badges/faces for key press.

■ **Parties**

Ask reporters where the parties are.

Go to booths rented by publications. Tell them you advertise and want an invitation.

Attend parties. Be low key.

If you've done your homework, the trade show public relations plan will go off smoothly.

Press Facilities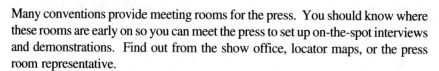

Many conventions provide meeting rooms for the press. You should know where these rooms are early on so you can meet the press to set up on-the-spot interviews and demonstrations. Find out from the show office, locator maps, or the press room representative.

If you have arranged interviews before the show that will be held at the press room, go there ahead of time so you will know how long it takes to get there from your booth. This way, you won't be late for your appointment and inconvenience the reporter. You'll also know how much privacy you will have, what facilities are available for demonstrating products and whether you'll need extra chairs. You should also check to see that exhibitors are allowed in the press room, as some shows limit entrance to only reporters.

The press room is reserved for the media to relax with their peers, read press kits, and conduct interviews with exhibitors. If lunch is served in this room, you will meet many reporters - some might welcome a demo or discussion.

Larger conventions may have a separate room for interviews. Comdex and PC Expo have working press rooms in which reporters can write their stories and send them to editors electronically. Don't even think of entering this room, as you will be seen as a pest. Monitors generally restrict access to this room to working press.

Press kit rooms are also hosted by larger conventions. See the following chapter for more information.

Press Kit Room ■

Imagine a lending library where editors can pick up your press kits at trade shows. It exists. It is called the press kit room. Nearly every trade show has an area in which vendors can display copies of their press kits for the press to pick up.

Your company can get a great deal of exposure by placing its press kits in these areas. The press kit room is an ideal marketing tool because you can reach reporters who might not stop by your booth because they don't know you or your products. When they read the press kits, however, they might be inspired to visit your booth to get more information, or they might have enough material to write their story from the press releases alone.

Larger shows have a separate press kit room. Smaller shows set up tables in the press room. The press kit room at large shows can be as big as football field, with tables laid out in long rows draped with colorful bunting and topped with thousands of press kits from hundreds of companies. The press kits are arranged in alphabetical order by the first letter of the company.

Your company can use several methods to make your kits stand out. Because most kits sit in huge piles on the table, you can make yours immediately different. Here are a few ways:

- Design a clear plastic box to hold your press kits. Place a flyer that displays the company name, logo or provocative message in a holder.

- Place your press kit in a book bag emblazoned with your company's name and logo.

- If the press won't recognize your name, don't place the press release in a folder. Instead, place your press kits on the table, naked. That way, the press will read your headline and make a decision. This is better than having reporters make their decision on the basis of whether they've heard about your company.

- If you are exhibiting in another vendor's booth, place a sticker on your press kit cover that says, "Visit us in the Widget World Booth - #1234" so the press can find you. Print the booth number on each press release as well. At a recent PC Expo, *Newsbytes* Reporter Dana Blankenhorn wanted to do follow up work on a product he saw at a successful press conference. He took the press kit from his bag and looked at the release. It didn't say which booth the company occupied. A company lost an opportunity.

Some shows have a person monitoring the entrance to the press room. This person's job is to keep attendees and vendors out and admit only the press. This ensures that only reporters - not competitors - pick up your kits. The press kit room monitors can take your press kits and place them on the proper table. Some show sponsors allow the vendor to perform this task.

It is easy to place your kits in the press kit room. Simply go there on the first day of the show (early!). The Consumer Electronics Show has monitors who place the kits on the tables. Comdex, PC Expo and Macworld let you put your kits on the tables. Bring a healthy supply of kits to store under the table. Check the supply on the table at least once a day and replenish the stock as necessary. If the show has two locations, you must bring press kits to each room.

By using these tips, you'll have a good chance of getting your message in front of the press.

Make Every Wall Tell Your Story

Every wall is a potential billboard that can publicize your company. Create a colorful flier that tells the time and location of your press conference, party, or special event. Post the flyer on bulletin boards and walls in the press room. Always bring scotch tape and push pins with you. That way you'll be prepared to attack any flat surface.

If the location of your event has not been assigned when you create the flyer, leave the room number blank. When you get the room assignment, write in the room name or number. The poster can tell people WHY to visit your booth. Be specific. For example:

Famous sports star will sign autographs at ABC Booth #123

Widget World demonstrates fastest widget in Booth #123

See the sample illustrations on the following pages.

This strategy has high impact and low cost. You merely need to design and print a flyer, which can be done inexpensively on a personal computer or at a copy shop which does desktop publishing. Total cost might be about $35 to design and print a few flyers.

Don't be a pest, though, by posting dozens of flyers. The show management might frown on this excess and tear down the mess. Remember: Post all bills.

World Class Software

will introduce

World Class Widget Maker

software to speed manufacturing

in Press Conference Room A-2

at 2:30 p.m. Thursday

Contact: James Scott, World Class Software, 800-xxx-xxxx
123 World Class Way, Silicon Siberia, CA 01234

World Class Software

will demonstrate

World Class Widget Maker

software to speed manufacturing

in Booth 227

Contact: James Scott, World Class Software, 800-xxx-xxxx
123 World Class Way, Silicon Siberia, CA 01234

How to Hunt for Reporters

When you go to the show on the first day, pretend you're a hunter. Just as a hunter looks for distinguishing colors on animals, you will want to look for distinct colors on the badges.

Everyone who attends a trade show wears a badge. Those badges tell you whether the person is an exhibitor, vendor, guest, distributor, or reporter. Each category is designated by a different color so you can tell who's who at a glance. Reporters generally have a ribbon attached to their badge that says "Press." What could be easier?

Badges and ribbons make your job easier because you'll spot reporter a mile away. Although their name and affiliation might be hard to read, at least you'll know who to approach.

Some people who wear press badges don't write a single word. They are fake reporters. They are ad sales people, consultants and others who can't help you get publicity. Imagine going through your whole pitch only to learn the pleasant, smiling, nodding person is really waiting for you finish so he can launch into an advertising sales pitch.

To maximize your time, you must distinguish between the real press and the fake press. The best advice is to know the reporters and magazines that are key to your marketing plan. You should be so familiar with the magazines and the reporter's pictures that you think you know them. If you've done your homework by creating media lists, calling the press and by reading everything in the magazines, you will avoid the fake press.

To separate the real press from the phonies, you must qualify the person to see if they can help you. The trick is to do it in such a way as to not offend a real reporter with whom you are not familiar. Here's how.

1. Introduce yourself.

2. Ask what they write about. If they say "new products," you are in business.

3. If they say "ad sales," you can make the situation work for you by asking the ad rep if your product category is on the magazine's editorial calendar. If it is, you can call the editor and pitch your product.

If you qualify reporters, you'll save time and energy that can be better applied on important writers.

Apply the rules of etiquette when tackling reporters:

- Introduce yourself briefly.
- Ask if they have 10 seconds to hear your positioning statement.
- Ask if they want to see a demo.
- Accompany reporters to booth, introduce to VIPs, supervise demo.
- Offer a press kit.
- Take business cards and write the follow up action to be taken (send software, press kit, call for interview, etc.).
- Thank them.

If reporters do not want to visit the booth, don't despair. They might be about to interview Bill Gates or attend a lavish party. Ask if they would like more information and note the responses on their business cards.

How to Give Demos That Have Editors Asking for More

Because reporters have a limited amount of time, you should be able to conduct three demos:

1. 30 seconds - executive summary
2. 1 minute - overview of key features/benefits
3. 5 minute - in-depth examination

The 30-second demo hits the highlights. It is used when reporters are on the run and don't have time to see the whole demo. You need to give them the most essential information up front. If you have done an outstanding job, they will ask for more information, come back later for an in-depth demo, ask for a press kit so they can write about the product, or ask for a product to review.

The five-minute demo is the in-depth demo. It is used for confirmed appointments, press conferences and truly interested reporters who have graduated from the 30-second demo and want more information. Five minutes should be enough time to cover the major topics in detail and still hold the reporter's attention.

The one-minute demo is good for the third-tier reporter. You want to be polite to these reporters, but you can't afford to tie up personnel. This demo should cover the major points, so they can write something.

You must create statements that clearly end the demo. This is important if you are pressed for time, as when an A list reporter visits a booth when you are demonstrating the product to a C list reporter. All demos can be cut short by asking the reporter if he would like you to send a review copy. You can also have another executive answer questions posed by the C list reporter.

Keep Requests from Falling in the Cracks

During the course of a convention, you will meet many reporters and analysts who will ask for a great many things: information, product, interviews, follow-up visits. How can you keep this information organized?

Here's a foolproof method. When you meet reporters, ask for their business cards and write their requests on the front or back of the cards. That way, you'll remember how to follow up and respond appropriately. You'll also have their names, addresses and phone numbers handy. Short descriptions will suffice. For example:

- Send software (note the format)
- Set phone interview with CEO re foreign trade

After a day or two, your pockets will bulge with cards and you'll be able to impress your supervisors as you flip through the cards. A stack of business cards carries weight - literally and figuratively.

You also want to collect business cards because freelancers, columnists and bureau chiefs don't always work out of the main editorial office of a publication. These cards will have their correct mailing addresses and phone numbers, so you can contact them speedily.

Keep your cards in your left pocket and other people's material in your right pocket to create an "In Pocket" and "Out Pocket."

Get Noticed by the Press

Willy Sutton, was asked why he robbed banks. He replied, "That's where the money is."

You go to press rooms because that's where the reporters are. One of the most effective guerrilla marketing strategies is to stand outside the press room and talk to reporters as they walk by.

This strategy is of key importance to companies that don't have booths because it positions you in a central meeting place where editors congregate. Even if you do have a booth, you should also spend time outside the press room. After all, the press wants to find a good story. Why not make it easy for them to find you?

If you follow this strategy, you must be careful to follow these rules of etiquette:

- Never interrupt a conversation.

- Never push yourself on reporters.

- Respect the reporter's time. He has other appointments and deadlines.

- Respect the reporter's privacy. The press room is the fortress of solitude.

If you have spare time, spend it near the press room. You'll find the greatest number of reporters congregate near the press room during breakfast and lunchtime.

Get Coverage by Piggybacking

To find reporters, go to a hot press conference sponsored by an industry leader. But don't go inside. That's bad form. Stand in the hallway and wait for the press to leave. When they're walking back to the show, you can see if they are interested in your product or service. This strategy has the advantage of letting somebody else collect reporters for you. You're piggybacking on their appeal.

For this strategy to be effective, you must know:

- The press by sight. You should be able to call out their names to can catch their attention.

- What pitch will interest them. If you've done your homework, you will know the right reporters.

You can find out about press conferences by asking the show office for a list of press conferences or by asking reporters where the action is.

That's guerilla marketing at its finest. That's how you can best use your time and your energies you want to maximize your exposure.

Train Your Staff to Work with Editors

Many times reporters will walk in and out of a booth with no one paying them the slightest attention. You know what will happen? Nothing. They will never write about that company.

Be proactive. When reporters walk within 10 feet of your booth, you should be prepared to talk to them. Don't be afraid to go up to reporters and say, "Are you interested in...?" or "I've got a product that does X,Y and Z, and our booth is right over here. Can I give you a one-minute demo?"

Since you can never know when reporters will visit your booth, you should take steps to ensure reporters are greeted and served in your absence. Everyone in your booth, from the booth manager to the people who are giving out product literature should look for reporters. When a reporter enters the booth, he or she should be directed to a press person or the person who is charged with dealing with reporters.

This tactic works well when you are in the middle of one important appointment and an important reporter drops by. An alert second in command should know exactly what to do: make an introduction, exchange a business card for a press kit, explain the product and supervise the demo.

Here's an easy way to reduce the chances of missing the press:

1. Create a list of the 25 most important reporters and their publications.

   - Read it to the booth personnel before the show.
   - Give them copies.
   - Place a copy under the desk in the booth reception area where staffers only can see it.

2. Create a procedure for dealing with the drop-by press:

   - Introduce yourself.
   - Call over the designated executive.
   - Position the product.
   - Ascertain their interest.
   - Supervise the demo.
   - Record follow-up requests.
   - Thank the reporter.

Booth Etiquette

Booth etiquette requires certain procedures. Never sit down. Sitting down makes it look like nothing is happening. No one will ever want to talk to you. No one goes up to someone who is sitting down.

Don't idly chat with other booth personnel. The sight of two well-dressed executives or sales people looks like a meeting. No one will interrupt a meeting. Certainly not a timid prospect.

- Eating.
- Drinking.
- Smoking.

These acts will ward off the press, as well as potential customers.

Body Language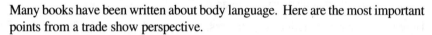

Many books have been written about body language. Here are the most important points from a trade show perspective.

- Talk to the person, not the monitor. It is too easy to get caught up in a demo by looking at the screen and talking to it. Maintain eye contact with the reporter.
- Raise your voice or you'll be drowned out by other people in the booth.
- Present an open posture. Folded arms and crossed legs are defensive positions that keep reporters on guard. To create intimacy and trust, let your arms hang at your sides and plant your feet about six inches apart.

Engross the reporter by asking questions. "Don't you agree?" "What do you think?" Keep the reporter involved.

How to Work a Party

When the show ends at 6:00 p.m., your work isn't done. This is where the fun starts. Parties begin.

Parties are very serious business at a trade show. You can probably get more done with the press at a party than during the show hours itself because the press is relaxed. They're agreeable.

There is an acknowledgement that your company has made it if you are seen at the right parties. If you know where the parties are, then you are obviously at a certain recognition level. The people who matter know that you're part of the infrastructure. That can be crucial to establishing and maintaining new contacts.

You can find out about parties by asking reporters with whom you are friendly. Don't ask strangers. That's gauche. Parties, after all, are supposed to be for those who have been invited. Don't expect a reporter to allow a stranger to crash a party.

Trade shows parties are be sponsored by magazines, exhibitors, and the press infrastructure. Magazine parties are held for advertisers but reporters usually attend. Call your ad rep before the show to get an invitation. You might be able to get an invitation if you didn't get one in the mail before the show if you stop by their booth. However, you run the risk of missing them while they are selling outside the booth. If you must crash, drop the names of reporters who will vouch for you if the bouncer calls them to verify your status.

Exhibitors parties are held by publishers, manufacturers, distributors for the press and customers. The press attends parties by the hot companies. Go to them.

One of the most famous press infrastructure parties occurs at Comdex. That one is hosted by columnist John Dvorak. The party has become an institution because of its secrecy. He tells only a few people on the inside about it and they tell only their friends, other insiders. Half the fun is finding out when and where the party will be held. If you find out, you will see the Who's Who of the PC computer industry. One Comdex party featured a shouting match between Microsoft Chairman Bill Gates and Paul Mace, founder of Mace Utilities, at an Atlanta hotel balcony as 100 people looked on. Gates left in a huff. If you were there, you were somebody.

Here's how to get invited: Find someone who is an insider and ask. If they know, you'll feel like an insider. If they don't know, you'll know where they rank. Because of the popularity of this party, people have been known to give false addresses for the party. Get confirmations from two sources.

Don't do a hard sell at a party. Remember, people are there to work, but in a relaxed format. You should be able to talk about topics other than your company and its products. This is a great opportunity to build rapport with the press.

Possible topics:

- Trends in your part of the industry.
- What the reporter found interesting at the show.
- What the reporter plans to write about in the coming months.
- What the reporter's opinion is of (fill in the blank).

The reporter will ask you what you do and what your company does. You can then relate the positioning statement and the prime benefits that would interest the reporter's audience. Ask how you can follow up on the reporter's needs.

How to Hold a Notable Press Conference

■

Press conferences for small companies are distinctly out of favor for these reasons:

- Competition from bigger companies steals reporters.
- Excitement on the show floor steals reporters.
- Reporters aren't interested in small companies.

Most publicity consultants advise against holding press conferences because only a few people will show up.

That's exactly why you should schedule a press conference.

- Your company and its message will be listed in the press conference roster. All reporters read this roster so you'll have another exposure to reporters. PC Expo lists all the press conferences on a billboard about 20 feet high with names printed in letters a foot high. This is good exposure and it doesn't cost a cent.

- The press might attend. You'll have a chance to tell them what is going on. Even if only one reporter attends, you can have a private talk and walk back to the booth for a demo.

- Never, never, never count the number of reporters when judging the effectiveness of the press conference. The quality and quantity of reporters affected by the message can transcend the number of people sitting in chairs.

You will want to schedule a press conference at small conventions because there is less competition. Follow this formula for staging a 15 minute press conference:

- Call to order, introduce yourself and the company (1 minute).

- Provide overview of new product (1 minute).

- Announce company positioning statement and background (2 minutes).

- Describe new product (3 minutes).

- Demonstrate new product (5 minutes).

- Questions (to completion).

- Thank everyone for attending. (10 seconds).

Bring press kits, promotional items and several layers of company exeuctives to the press conference. Collect reporters' business cards when they arrive so you can follow up after the show.

Promote Products
and Services on Panels

Most trade shows have panel sessions that feature prominent industry persons who deliver speeches. These panels present an opportunity for your executives to promote the product. While you cannot pitch your product from the podium, there are many good reasons for speaking on a panel:

- The placement will elevate the company in the eyes of everyone who attends the session or who reads about the session in the show guide. By sitting next to the same people who are shaping the industry, you will benefit from their aura. People will perceive you and your company to be in the same league as those prime players.

- You probably will be allowed to share your views on the future of the industry as it relates to your industry segment, so you can shed light on your company and its plans.

- You will be recognized.

Getting invited to speak on a panel is only the first step. Remember, your objective is for the press to see and hear you. You all remember the sound that a tree makes in the forest if there is no one around to listen.

For media exposure, follow these steps:

- Call or write the key press and tell them when you will speak and what you will say.

- Confirm attendees.
- Speak to reporters before and after the talk.
- Distribute truly newsworthy remarks to the press.
- Send prepared remarks to reporters after the show.

Getting Chosen to Speak on a Panel

Many people want to sit on those few select panel seats. This chapter will help you understand how to get chosen to serve on a panel.

The conference sponsor selects a board of editors and analysts to create the program. Usually these are the same people every year. You can find out who they are by looking at last year's program guide.

Call these experts and tell them who you are and that you would like to help them create the panel for the next show. Suggest topics. They will benefit from hearing your recommendations, as long as those suggestions are not self-serving. To build credibility with the program planner, be prepared to send the following material:

- Biography.
- Photo (needed for catalog).
- Articles and books you have written.
- Articles written about you.
- Testimonial letters from other speaking assignments or clients.

Most panels follow the broad theme of "future trends" in the industry. Use this ammunition when you call the experts. You might ask them if they have chosen the topic for next year's show. If they have, what is it?

Then suggest how your can help add zest and information to the panel. Make sure you have compelling reasons for them to select you. State your background, your view of the industry, your insight into future events. Tell them that you are an expert and act the part.

If the panel has been set (as some panels are with old cronies and the same faces), you aren't completely out of luck. If all else fails, go to the panel chair the day of the talk and see if he needs an extra speaker to replace one who has failed to show up. Also, your topic might be more relevant in light of changes in the industry. In that case, your talk will be highly valued.

How to Prepare for the Speaker's Role

After you have landed the assignment to speak on a panel, find out what will be expected of you. Ask these questions and you will be able to make a better presentation and save yourself from wasting energy.

- How long is your talk?
- Will there be questions from the moderator or attendees?
- Will there be audio visual equipment, overhead projectors? Computers?
- When should you arrive at the room?
- Will there be a meeting with other speakers beforehand?
- What topics are off limits?
- What topics will be covered by other speakers?
- What is the speaking order? (Important because you will know whether information has already been presented.)

Prior planning will prevent disasters.

Follow this Time Schedule for Speaking:

1 year before show	Find out the speaking planners.
Nine months before show	Call speaking planners and discuss topics, gain seat on panel.
Three months before show	Write an outline of remarks and submit to panel chairperson.
One month before show	Review outline, write about main topics to be covered.
	Practice speech in front of executives, publicist.
	Time the speech. Tell the press your topic.
	Copy outline, prepared remarks, transparencies.
Day of the speech	Send copies of speech to reporters via Business Wire of PR Newswire and your press list.

Create Your Own Panel

After you have developed your position in the industry, you might be asked to create a panel. This exceptional opportunity might also come your way if you target a unique panel idea to the sponsor of a small show that does not have a formal panel of advisors.

Creating your own panel is a very exciting opportunity to present yourself favorably.

A good panel has one goal: it helps the audience better understand the topic under discussion. Your credibility will rise or fall on how successful you are in meeting your audience's needs. You should not promote your services, company or products directly. You will benefit from the aura of credibility that surrounds your role as the chairperson. In the short term, you reap benefits by having important vendors and reporters contact you after the session because you are now a recognized expert on the topic.

In the long run you can use this aura to enhance your biography and as a leverage tool when talking to the press ("As I mentioned on the Comdex panel I chaired...").

Get Exposure From the Audience

Even if you don't get seated on the speaking panel, you should go the session so you can take advantage of the guerilla marketing tactics to benefit your company.

After the speaker has finished, questions are taken from the floor. Ask an intelligent question. You will benefit from people recognizing you. You will also gain credibility with the other speakers and panel chair.

After the session, meet the chair and other speakers. Tell them of your background — quickly — and offer your services for the next panel.

Chapter 4 How to Follow Up

Follow up

Your job isn't over when the show ends. This section will explore the activities you should perform after the show. Here is an outline of suggested activities.

- **Follow up**

    Send thank you notes to interviewers.

    Send press kits to new contacts.

    Send review products to editors.

- **Call media who did not attend the show.**

    Pitch news story.

    Pitch review.

    Pitch feature articles and/or case histories.

- **Read publications for mentions of your articles.**

- **Obtain permission to reprint reviews.**

- **Arrange a press tour to key media.**

Why You Must Follow up

Now you have come back from the show armed with editor's business cards. You must follow up to maintain the momentum. Remember, the same editors who liked your product also talked to 20 other companies that grabbed their attentions. You need to keep your company in front of reporters so they won't forget about your products. You've done too much work to let the whole program stop.

Remember, getting things done is key. You must have the ability to follow through if you are to succeed. The strength of the whole program depends on these steps.

Thank-You Notes Improve Response

The first thing you should do after a convention is send thank you letters to everyone you talked to.

These notes serve several purposes. They:

- Keep your name in front of the reporter.

- Remind reporters of your meeting.

- Answer questions raised at the meeting.

- Introduce demo products.

- Demonstrate good manners.

The writing process should not take long, especially if you use the mail merge function on your word processor. These notes can be short and to the point. However, they must be personalized. Interject notes about when you met reporters (at the booth, at a party, waiting for the bus, on the plane ride home) or other interesting tidbits that will make you stand out in their minds (attended same college, worked for same boss, allergic to same foods). The more personalized the letters, the less likely they will be seen as impersonal form letters. Done correctly, your letters will help you build personal relationships with editors. The note should say something like the ones found on the following pages. Modify the letters to fit your needs. These samples are meant as guidelines only.

The major points are:

- Use the person's name, not "Dear Editor", so the letters look personal.

- Politely ask them to act. (for example, "Can I provide you with any help in answering questions for your article.")

- Don't threaten, coax, cajole.

- Don't etalk about buying advertising space (a cardinal rule of journal ism is that editorial and advertising departments are separate).

Send the product. Coordinate this activity with your company's shipping department so they can send all the material (product, press releases, letter) quickly. Seize the moment.

Sample Cover Letter Accompanying Product for Review

DATE

Name
Title
Periodical
Address
City, State Zip

Dear_____,

I enjoyed meeting you at COMDEX and demonstrating MY PRODUCT to you. Isn't it nice to know you can meet interesting people while standing on the taxi line!

Your readers should be interested in this product because it solves the problem of BENEFIT # 1.

As you requested, I am sending you a copy of THE PRODUCT to you in this package. I will call you in two weeks to see how you like it.

Please call me if I can answer any questions.

Sincerely yours,

Daniel Janal
President

DSJ/rrr

Sample letter: When the Product is Not Ready to Ship

DATE
Name
Title
Periodical
Address
City, State Zip

Dear_____,

I enjoyed meeting you at COMDEX and demonstrating MY PRODUCT to you. Isn't it nice to know you can meet interesting people while standing on the taxi line!

Your readers should be interested in this product because it solves the problem of BENEFIT # 1.

As you requested, I will send you a copy of the product when it ships on DATE.

Please call me if I can answer any questions.

Sincerely yours,

Daniel Janal
President
DSJ/rrr

Sample letter: To Schedule a Demonstration at the Editor's Office

DATE

Name
Title
Periodical
Address
City, State Zip

Dear_____,

I enjoyed meeting you at COMDEX and demonstrating MY PRODUCT to you. Isn't it nice to know you can meet interesting people while standing on the taxi line!

Your readers should be interested in this product because it solves the problem of BENEFIT # 1.

As you suggested, I will call you shortly to arrange a time to meet you in your offices to demo the product.

Please call me if I can answer any questions.

Sincerely yours,

Daniel Janal
President

DSJ/rrr

DATE

Name
Title
Periodical
Address
City, State Zip

Dear_____,

I enjoyed meeting you at COMDEX and demonstrating MY PRODUCT to you. Isn't it nice to know you can meet interesting people while standing on the taxi line!

Your readers should be interested in this product because it solves the problem of BENEFIT # 1.

As you remember, you wanted to know if the product does REFERENCE. I have spoken to our MANAGEMENT/TECHNICAL DEPARTMENT and the answer is ANSWER.

Please call me if I can answer any questions.

Sincerely yours,

Daniel Janal
President

DSJ/rrr

Following Up with Other Media

Not every publication can send a reporter to a show. You need to call those editors and tell them your story. If you haven't done this before the show, you should do so now.

Your goals are to pitch these stories:

- News story announcing new product.
- Review the product.
- Include product in roundup of similar products.
- Convince magazine to reprint the case history.
- (Optional) Schedule a demo at their offices.

You now have the advantage of having refined your pitch from the trade show and pre-show calling. You have the confidence in knowing how to create interest and convince reporters to write about your company and its products.

SECTION 3

How to Hire, Fire and Inspire an Agency

Should high tech companies hire a public relations agency or assign the responsibility to a staff member. This section will discuss objectively the pros and cons of each option.

The Case for Hiring an Agency

PR agencies provide companies with the opportunity to hire experts for a specific task at a pre-defined rate. When you hire an agency, you can be reasonable assured of working with professionals who understand the press, the industry and - in short time - your company.

Your company also will benefit from the air of professionalism and the quality of their writing, pitching and placement skills. Your company also will bask in the collective sunshine of the PR agency's credibility with the media and the public.

Heavyweights at the PR agency can lend their credibility and personal contacts with the media to present your company's message clearly and accurately.

The Case for In-House Personnel

Many fine publicists provide professional service for companies and live quite nicely without outside help. The staff performs its job admirably, provides a high degree of professional service and maintains contact with the media that lead to solid results.

PR agencies can save your company time and money when promoting products and services. For the company that has a PR department, an agency can provide oversight activities and perform special projects that the company lacks the expertise or manpower. For companies that lack PR departments, the agency can used as an arm of the marketing or sales departments.

International companies, start-ups and companies involved in down-sizing can benefit from the experience of the public relations agency. Local agencies might be able to provide expertise in fields that international concerns are unfamiliar. Start-ups and down-sized companies can benefit from the extra personnel an agency offers - without taking on additional costs of salaries, benefits, desk space and office support.

How to Hire an Agency

The best way to hire an agency - as with any personal services - is to ask for recommendations. You also might notice a company getting a lot of publicity. Find out who does their public relations.

Contact at least two agencies so you can get a feel for the wide range in which different companies work. You will find a difference in working style, personalities and temperament. Select the one that best meets your style.

Any agency should be happy to provide an initial consultation for free and provide a statement of qualifications. If you want to receive a detailed proposal, some agencies might charge for this service. Their rationale is that the work takes a great deal of time, is speculative, and the ideas are proprietary. However, some agencies will go to the expense of performing such a proposal. Be fair and only ask for proposals from companies in which you are truly interested.

A letter of agreement or formal contract is necessary to begin service. The documents should spell out the price of the service, length of service, renewal procedures, and confidentiality. Expenses are billed directly to the company, either at cost or at a markup of approximately 16.5 percent per year to cover the administrative and finance charges.

Include a clause stating your company owns the copyright on all material the agency produces.

Create Relationships by Setting Goals

To ensure a good working relationship when you hire an agency, identify the goals and the responsibilities of the agency and the company. By referring to the Goal Setting Worksheet in this book, you will be able to set on goals that are identifiable, measurable and attainable. These goals will keep everyone on track, especially if they create a time line of activities. Of course, not every goal can be met for a variety of legitimate reasons. However, this blueprint should be used to keep everyone on track.

The company should make one person responsible for dealing with the public relations agency. This person will act as a clearing house for the company: approve press release, find company personnel the agency needs to interview, sign off on all invoices and assign administrative tasks.

How to Evaluate Services

Daily contact with between the agency and the company will help ensure that work is performed on time and produces the desired results. Agencies should send periodic reports to the company to show they are active. The minimum acceptable term is once a month, usually with the invoice. The report should include an executive summary of services performed, a complete statement of activities including successes, pending matters and failures. Copies of articles should be sent to the client as soon as the agency finds them. Additional copies should be attached to the monthly report.

The company contact person should copy the report and send it to others responsible for marketing and sales so that everyone knows what activities are being performed. The other staffs might find uses for the public relations material (news and reviews) being generated. Key decision makers also will realize that the agency is working on their behalf - not asleep at the wheel. Monthly activity reports help the agency keep the client happy.

How to Set a Budget

Public relations agency fees vary greatly. Some agencies work on an hourly or project basis. Others require a six-month minimum commitment with a significant monthly retainer, usually $5-6000 with the understanding that the fee will grow.

The rule of thumb is that PR budgets are 1 percent of sales. By contrast, advertising budgets are 10 percent of sales. Depending on your industry of project, the budget will vary. Whatever the figure, agree on the terms in advance to avoid misunderstanding in the future. If your company has a policy, such as not using Federal Express or traveling first class, make these procedures known in advance to avoid turmoil later.

How to Inspire an Agency

Agencies work best when they are part of the team. Treat agency members as you would your most trusted employees. In fact, they are. They take your message to the media, so they must know every ramification of what they say, so that they don't upset plans to which they have not been apprised. Invite them to company parties, picnics and staff meetings so that they develop personal relationships and feelings of loyalty to your company, its staff and the program.

How to Fire an Agency

If the relationship does not work out, the agency can be fired under the terms of the contract's dissolution clause. No matter what the problem, keep the relationship on a professional level as you might need each other in the future.

About the Author

Daniel S. Janal
Public Relations Consultant
Author
Speaker
Workshop leader

Daniel S. Janal is President of JANAL COMMUNICATIONS, a Danville, California based public relations agency specializing in computer hardware and software products; and JANAL TRAINING SEMINARS, which help businesses empower their employees with the skills to market their products more effectively through publicity, advertising and direct mail.

Dan has written numerous articles on business productivity, communications, computer usage and home office/telecommuting. He is the author of the best-selling software program *Publicity Builder.*

Dan's public relations consulting background spans more than a decade, including stints with New York City public relations agencies. He formed his own agency in 1986. He has handled successful publicity campaigns for such companies as Grolier Electronic Publishing, Prentice-Hall Home Software, Commodore International, America Online (formerly QuantumLink) and many others.

An award-winning newspaper reporter, Dan worked for Gannett newspapers in West Virginia, Florida and New York as a general assignment reporter, news editor and business news editor. He won writing awards from the Hearst Foundation, the Greater Orlando Press Club and the National Teacher's Association/Florida Teaching Profession. He has contributed articles to InfoWorld, Computer Dealer, Compute! and CompuServe.

Dan has presented portions of his Janal Training Seminars at conferences sponsored by the Software Publishers Association, the Public Relations Society of America, the Learning Annex and Apple Developers Conference. Dan is available to speak at your company's meetings and lead its workshops.

He is a graduate of Northwestern University's Medill School of Journalism, where he earned bachelor's and master's degrees in journalism.

Dan can be contacted at 510-831-0900 or 657 Doral Drive, Danville, CA 94526 for assistance with your company's or organization's publicity programs.

An open letter to readers of *How to Publicize High Tech Products and Services*

FM: Daniel Janal
RE: Working together in the future

A few days ago, while I was walking through the aisles of a major trade show, a young woman stopped me and introduced herself. She said she recognized me by the picture on my publicity book. She told me she had learned many new publicity strategies that helped her get press coverage.

Then she said something that knocked me on the floor. She had just given a PR project — *it would have been perfect for me* — to someone else.

"Why didn't you call me?" I asked.

"I didn't know you consulted with small companies outside of Silicon Valley!" she replied.

Let me tell you, this has happened before. I feel like I'm watching the same scene from a bad movie over and over again.

So that's why I'm writing to you now. While it is true that more than 4,000 people bought my books, and larger, well-known companies are clients, I also work with smaller startups. My fees are less than those of other agencies because I keep my overhead low. I work out of my home yet I serve clients all over the country.

All I want you to do is STOP. Think of DAN JANAL the next time you have a publicity or marketing communications project.

I love the excitement of bringing a new product to market — or helping revitalize an existing product. If this describes your company, I want to talk with you about your publicity and marketing communications needs. If you're thinking of hiring a public relations agency for a long-term commitment, or a one-time project (like writing a press kit), or having me train your publicity staff, please call me at 510-831-0900 for a FREE consultation!

I want to show you how to unlock the power of publicity to put extra profits in your pocket. I can offer a lot. Let's go to work now!

P.S. Call me at 510-831-0900 before noon Pacific Time and I'll fax you a FREE copy of my latest time-saving tool — the Fool-Proof Positioning Statement. If you enjoyed the time-saving and thought-provoking worksheets in the book, you'll love this new one! It's yours free as a gift!

Let's Get VERTICAL!

Are you selling a specialized application or product? These "vertical market applications" present a whole new set of publicity programs that many large PR agencies can't – and won't – handle.

That's because they like to turn out PR campaigns like cookie cutters. "One program fits all" is their motto. That way they can amortize their expenses and their experience. Also, these smaller products don't require the PR campaigns that make the cash register jingle.

At Janal Communications, we look at programs differently. We like the challenge of placing articles in Construction Today as much as we do in PC Magazine. We love writing case histories and application stories– and convincing editors to print these stories *word-for-word*. The more esoteric the application, the better job we'll do. Do you have a program that tracks nuclear waste and handles the SARA reporting requirements? We speak your language.

Call Dan Janal at 510-831-0900 today to discuss your special needs. At Janal Communications, you'll get a publicity program that is a custom, tailored fit.